In Pursuit of Leo
A Memoir

Grace Holmes Tobey Lockwood Paine

181 PUBLISHING
ATLANTA, GEORGIA

In Pursuit of Leo: A Memoir

Published by 181 Publishing
Atlanta, Georgia

The off-road vehicle logo is a trademark of 181 Publishing.

The author has recreated events, locales and conversations from her memories of them. In order to maintain their anonymity, the names of individuals and places may be changed in some instances or identifying characteristics and details such as physical properties, occupations and places of residence altered.

Cover Design & Tobey Family Tree: Jess Creatives
(*www.jesscreatives.com*)

ISBN: 978-0-9962287-5-6

The *Tobey* Family Tree

married Frank: 9/30/1983
Maureen Fitzgerald

Thomas Tobey Paine
2/26/1960

Linda Sue Paine-Powe
101/3/1954

Donald Wells
11/2/1944

Russ Paine, IV
11/17/1952

Robert E. Wells
7/21/1938 - 11/25/2011

Kenneth C. Wells
1/8/1951

married Frank: 5/26/19
Johanne Thompso
3/10/1929

married Janet: 9/4/1937
Howard W. Wells
2/7/1912 - 7/1/1973

Frank Tobey Pain
10/19/1927 - 10/19/19

James Russell Paine, III
10/24/1924 - 3/3/1944

Janet Helen Lockwood
9/20/1917 - 9/29/2001

married Grace: 5/3/1923
James Russell Paine, II
2/9/1891 - 7/13/1970

married Grace: 2/14/1917
Demetrius L. Lockwood
10/14/1892 - 5/21/1919

Grace Tobey Paine
8/3/1896 - 2/13/1989

Helen Doris Tobey
11/16/1899 - 8/5/1917

Frank W. Tobey *married* Linda Holmes Tobey
1869 - 5/15/1931   *4/9/1868 - 6/5/1945*

Foreword

When I was a kid, my parents would round up my brother, sisters, and me for what we referred to as Dad's Memorial Day Tour. This event didn't happen every year, but it happened consistently from the time I was in grade school, through high school, and into my college years.

The tour would begin at our home in Oswego, New York, and travel south, stopping at several cemeteries along the way. My mom would prepare flower arrangements in advance and, at each stop, we would place flowers on the headstone of a family member, and my parents would tell us stories of that particular person. When I was a little girl, I didn't know any of the people whose graves we visited. Both of my grandfathers passed away before I was born, and as a child, I had not yet suffered great loss. It wasn't until I was in high school and my Grandma Jan passed away, that I was able to join the storytelling with my own first-hand accounts.

Every year, our memorial tour culminated at historic Oakwood Cemetery in Syracuse, New York. We would pile out of our station wagon, and carefully make our way through the bending paths of Oakwood Cemetery, passing great monuments along the way, until we came to a simple stone bench. Engraved in the side of the bench was the name TOBEY on one side and LOCKWOOD PAINE on the other.

These were familiar names, the centerpieces of many of my dad's stories. However, the details of these yarns seemed complex and remained convoluted in my head until recently. My dad would sit us down on the bench, feet dangling over the side, and begin, "Your Grandma Jan's mother, Mama Grace, married your great-grandfather Demetrius..." Before long, I would be asking questions like, "Wait, *which* Frank?" and "How many Russell's *were* there?"

The truth is that Mama Grace's story was complex because it was interwoven with the stories of her parents and sister, her lovers, and her children who she loved dearly, and far too many of these stories ended abruptly. The little bench we were sitting on had found its way to Oakwood Cemetery because Mama Grace needed a place to sit with those she loved, and hoped that in the future, other family would come and do the same. I would sit there and wonder how one person could endure so much heartache.

I've carried my dad's stories with me for years, always with a wavering degree of clarity. Things would become most clear when my dad pulled out old family photo albums and showed us pictures of women holding children, boys in Tarzan suits playing on the beach, and men standing next to classic cars. But then the pictures would go back in a box and again I would find myself playing a mental game of who was who.

In fall 2014, my cousin Bob, my husband Tim, and I were having dinner together while Bob was visiting Atlanta on business. Bob is the oldest son of my dad's oldest brother, and I am the youngest child in my family. Due to the age span between Uncle Bob and my dad, my cousin "Bobby" is closer in age to my dad's generation than to mine; I grew up playing with his kids at family reunions and summer get-togethers.

Between bites of pizza, I told Bob that I wanted one of my upcoming writing projects to be interviewing my dad about the stories he had told us when we were young. The accounts were so rich with history, love, and tragedy, it saddened me to think about them fading away as the generations of our family extend forward. In response, Bob nonchalantly said, "Mama Grace had an affinity for writing too. I believe I have a manuscript she wrote at my house, with some other things that came from dad's." My eyes grew big and I just about dropped my fork in my lap. I asked Bob if there was any possibility of locating it and he agreed to keep his eyes open for it the next time he was in that particular section of storage.

On a rainy October afternoon in 2015, I missed a phone call from Bob. It was followed quickly with a text message that said, "Guess what we finally found?" and included an image of a white sheet of paper, with "by Grace Holmes Tobey Lockwood Paine" in a faded, black typewritten font. By the end of the week, Bob had scanned all 94 pages and sent me a digital copy of the manuscript. For several years, Bob has worked for a company that specializes in printing and scanning technology, and he was pleased to inform me about the details of the scanning process. I am grateful that due to his knowledge in this area, Bob was able to take a faded, yellowed manuscript and make it legible for me to read and transcribe.

That Saturday morning, I went to a local print shop and printed *In Pursuit of Leo*, Mama Grace's original title for the work. Walking out of the store that day, a stack of 94 warm pages in my hands, I was elated – filled with pride and gratitude to be holding the words of a woman that, since childhood, I had so desperately longed to know. I went directly to my favorite coffee shop and, over two cups of coffee, read the entire manuscript from beginning to end. It was beautiful and triggered a wide variety of emotions. I laughed at her tales of mischief, pondered life's bigger questions of life and death, and cried more than I would like to admit; tears of joy for the clarity I finally gained and tears of sorrow for finally understanding the tragedies and losses that took place.

Over and over in my reading, one phrase kept coming to mind, "Now I understand..." I finally understood why Grandma Jan loved for my sisters and I to play the violin for her when she visited. I finally understood where my family got their wonderful sense of humor and why my heart feels at peace when I'm near the water. I finally understood the reason my dad is strong even in the face of adversity, and why he and my mother have been unwaveringly in love for so many years. Over and over, I saw the story God has traced through our family, beginning with a young pharmacist and his wife in 1800's Rochester.

I went home and began to sketch out a family tree, tracing from Frank W. Tobey to my father's generation. My cousin Bob again became a resource, patiently answering the questions I had about the details. At the end of one conversation, he suggested I contact Linda Paine-Powell. Although I only remembered meeting Linda once, my parents always speak fondly of her and I felt confident she would be excited to help me explore the Paine side of our family tree. She did not disappoint. The majority of the photos in this book came from the collection of albums she has preserved in her home.

Speaking with Bob and Linda about Mama Grace confirmed for me what had been evident in my dad's stories and what is written on every page of what you now hold in your hands: That Mama Grace felt deeply for her family and friends, that she was intelligent and honest, and that her ability to laugh had no end. Linda shared with me a picture from one of Mama Grace's birthday parties in her later years. On the back of the picture is written, "The '100th' birthday party in Washington." The story goes that a member of the family (Linda believes on the Wells' side) wrote to the White House, informing them that Grace Tobey Paine was celebrating her 100th year. The year was 1980, and it was actually only her 84th birthday. Mama Grace got endless joy out of this ruse played on her behalf.

In his novel *My Grandmother Asked Me to Tell You She's Sorry*, Fredrick Backman writes, "Having a grandmother is like having an army. This is a grandchild's ultimate privilege: knowing that someone is on your side, always, whatever the details. Even when you are wrong. Especially then, in fact." There is something special about relationships that skip from generation to generation. I see it in the way my dad, Ken, talks about summer days at Fair Haven with his grandmother, and in the way my own mother plays with my four-year-old niece Olivia.

In Pursuit of Leo is the story of a community. It is a testament to the necessary chaos of Sunday dinners together and sunsets at the beach. It is filled with the laughter of practical jokes and of dancing to live music. It is the unraveling of what happens in our hearts when we lean into our closest relationships. It is a memorial to those who left home behind to serve in our military during some of the world's most turbulent days, and a note of gratitude to those who vigilantly waited for their return.

Of course, these are all side themes of *In Pursuit of Leo's* original intent of one woman to tell her story to her family. It is a love story. A lineage. An explanation. In some ways, it may raise as many questions as it provides answers. These questions come as no surprise to the author. It is because of them that there is a little bench in the middle of Oakwood Cemetery. It is my privilege to invite you to come, have a seat, and hear the story of my great-grandmother Grace Holmes Tobey Lockwood Paine.

Stephanie (Wells) Whitacre
Christmas, 2015

PART I

I wrote the first part of this manuscript, with the intention of calling it My Story, *for my three children, if they should prove to be interested. This first part was found among some papers that were dated 1955. I do not really know the date of its writing. Much earlier, I think. The account is authentic.*

Chapter 1

The brick walls of the grocery store were not bright and shining but held the solidness of practical usage. Up five steps placed across the corner, one could enter and greet the grocer arrayed in his white canvas apron. The store was pungent with food and news items. One was led to become quite garrulous in this atmosphere of expansiveness. The position of the steps showed the modern trend, for modern times it was; being 1896, and the gay nineties were already in full swing. The steps straddled Tremont Street and Plymouth Avenue. Plymouth Avenue was one of the show streets of Rochester, New York, squaring away to the south from Main Street. Here there were stately ornate houses surrounded by filigreed iron fences, shadowed by tall trees. The stabling barns in the rear housed the high-stepping horses and the fringed carriages. There were blocks of brown stone fronts, so fashionable then, making unnatural crowding in this city of spaces. But then, the higher one could go in a house, the more fashionable it seemed. One's drawing room could not be placed in close proximity to the dining room nor sullied by the kitchen. South of the brownstones a small center supplied the needs of the locality. Opposite the Tremont side of the grocery was the local drugstore. Across on Plymouth were the penny candy and tobacco store and general notions shop. Such camaraderie existed between them that, when shopping, there was always time to go from one to the other across the cobble stone street.

On this day there was a whisper as the wind rose; a whisper of something new. The air had been hot and humid this third of August; the feeling of concentrated struggle as if the very elements were attempting to burst thru to life. The sun was still above the horizon but its brightness was beginning to dim. At this moment, a young man of 27 came running down the stairway to the street from the living quarters of the store. He darted out the door in great haste, clad in shirtsleeves and a row white vest, hurriedly fastening the row of brass buttons that decorated the vest's front.

The man ran up the five steps of the grocery. Putting the small handled pail on the counter, he cried joyfully, "It's here! We have a girl! The Doc wants my wife to have some warm milk. A pint will do." The grocer smiled. It was an old story with him, yet in the telling it became forever new. A new life! What would it mean to this one? He remembered when he too could have told the same story with the same excitement.

"Doc say the wife is all right?" The young man nodded with a smile and, grabbing the handle of the milk pail, rushed out of the store. Wife all right? Why, of course! Why not? But it flashed thru his mind, "Jumping Jehoshaphat – that wife of his! Light brown hair and blue eyes. Not so strong physically perhaps, as these months had been hard on her - but what an intellect! Independent thinker too."

4

He smiled proudly as he ran up the stairs. "Here it is, Doctor. My wife is all right?" he added as if in echo to his thoughts. Assured, he stroked his mustache and walked in where his wife lay. "She does look a bit done up," he mused and looked at the tiny daughter asleep upon her arm. "You're a brick, Linda," he said. "Looks like any other youngster, I guess." But did she? Something flashed from that small form to him and within he answered as to a resonant chord. Thus came about the binding of two people with a deep sympathetic understanding which was to hold thru the years until his death.

The room glowed with the fading sun. His wife was fast asleep now. The child stirred and grunted. He mused on into darkness until arising, he looked out the window into the night. The moon was riding the clouds full and bright. It smiled down at him and in age-old wisdom seemed to say, "I had a part in this."

Facing Tremont Street, next to the grocery store, was an old brick house covered with ivy vines. A small yard separated the two in which a broken fountain sprinkled water on three bathing birds. The little side porch was recessed and hidden by hanging vines. On the top step, a child of two years old sat eating bread and milk out of a bowl. Every day she sat there, always at the same place and nearly at the same time. Real birds flitted down to the fountain to share with the stone ones. The child was fascinated! "Auntie Peart, Auntie Peart, why do they fly away?" she called. "Because they want to see the world, Grace," Auntie Peart responded. "What's the world?" the child persisted. "Don't think I know myself. Do you want to go up and see Aunt Effie now?"

The child put her bowl upon the steps and went into the dining room, which was all set up formally, as if company was expected at any moment. Then she went thru the sitting room but not into the stiff-chaired parlor separated by tasseled portieres. This she only looked into. It was the forbidden room. Why, she didn't know! There was no one there. Only the marble top table, the long golden mirror, the horsehair chairs, and a corner full of plants.

Out into a hallway and up some carpeted stairs to Aunt Effie's room she went. Here you could look out the window at the birds in the fountain if you were careful with the curtains. Aunt Effie lay in bed as you were accustomed to seeing her. She was loving and affectionate and always looked so pretty and smelled so nice. Even the room was pretty. You were happy here, happier than anywhere except at Papa's drugstore.

Papa's store had a sign across the top. You couldn't read it yet, but it said to the neighborhood in general, "Frank W. Tobey, Pharmacist." The store could only be gone into at special times when Papa helped you across the street. You couldn't remember Momma going there. She always said she was too busy or too tired. Papa seemed to understand, but sometimes he looked too thoughtful. But you weren't thinking of that yet.

Today, Papa had you by the hand. You were on the way to Papa's store. "How's my goldilocks?" he asked as you walked up and down the five steps. "Good!" You managed a half dance, a half skip. "What's it to be today?" "A stwawbury soda," you answered as he held your hand crossing the street. It was always a "stwawbury" soda! The straw you crushed and bent as you looked around you. Shelves and shelves of bottles; white bottles and brown bottles, small bottles and large bottles. A fancy one by your side contained rock candy. The marble topped counter was very interesting. It had a cigar lighter with a flame. Papa said to stay away from that but it only made it more fascinating.

Perched upon a high stool with a metal frame, it took you nearly an hour to drink the soda. Finally, he said, "Come on, my 'stwawbury' blond – back to Momma." It was good to hang onto Papa's hand as you climbed the dark stairway. Momma seemed unhappy and disturbed. "Cheer-up, Linda," he said, "It's not too long now. Everything will be all right." There was something so vaguely unhappy and frustrated about Momma. You sensed it and it saddened you. You walked over and put your head in her lap. Why do Momma's sometime seem so far away?

The doll lay on the floor with its dress over its face. You picked it up and hugged and kissed it and, dragging it by one arm, you went over to see Auntie Peart and to find out whether Aunt Effie was in or out of bed.

"Tomorrow you'll be three," said Auntie Peart. "Aunt Effie wants a party. You come over. Your mother isn't feeling well. Someday you'll have a little brother or sister." "I don't want a brother or sister," you said, "I want to live with you and Papa."

"Margaret," said Aunt Effie, "Let's fix her all up sweet for the party." So your golden hair was washed and brushed and tied with ribbons. Excitement grew in the air. Parties you had found meant trips to Papa's store and maybe a present. And now a real party! Aunt Effie went out in the yard which she seldom did. Auntie Peart said she was too del-li-cut. It sounded very nice, especially when you smelled so good.

"Linda," Effie called, do come over. "Oh, I can't," said Momma. "Yes, you can, Linda. Come over to the party." "Well, I'll see." You sang a little after that – something about a froggy who would a-wooing go. Papa had taught it to you.

Today was the party. Aunt Effie was downstairs again. Auntie Peart fixed all the things on the table. It was the prettiest table you'd ever seen. You thrilled to it as you always were to thrill to beauty all your life.

You were placed high on books on a chair and the pretty flowers were right in front of you. Momma sat across from you. Auntie Peart came in from the kitchen. Aunt Effie patted your head. Your eyes danced with excitement. The door opened and there was Papa who brought "stwawbury" sodas and ice cream. The cake had candles on it. You were told to blow. Papa laughed. You felt merry and gay. Even Momma seemed to like it. She said, "That's a wonderful thing you did, Auntie Peart." "She's such a sweet one," was the reply. You glowed with the appreciation.

"Star" Mosher lived across the street. He was five and could walk alone across the street to see you. One day he came as you were swinging on the ornate iron gate and your foot was caught in a small space between an iron leaf and a stem. Tears came down your face.

"You're a baby," said Star. "I'm not a baby," you said emphatically, crying all the harder. Auntie Peart put her head out the door. "What's the matter, Grace? Star, why didn't you help her?" "Because she's a baby," said Star, departing quickly.

The leaves came down and it was fun burrowing into them. They became enchanted houses all of pretty colors. You wondered what you'd find when you came out the other side of the piles. Sometimes Star came over and buried you. Auntie Peart would put her head out the door to give a smile.

The days went by and then came the winter's snow. Aunt Effie knit you a pair of mittens and Papa built you a sled. Papa took you out on Plymouth Avenue and ran with you on the sled. You laughed in glee. Papa was wonderful! You sobered when you thought of Momma, but you couldn't understand.

Then one day, it all happened so fast. Papa said, "Get your nightie and your toothbrush, Goldilocks. You're going to sleep at Auntie Peart's tonight." That was the big "adventure" Papa had been talking to you about. Auntie Peart put on your nightie and Aunt Effie put on the pretty smell and you were tucked in, too excited to go to sleep.

In the morning, on November 15, you awoke to find you had a baby sister. Auntie Peart took you over. You stood on one foot, and then on the other, looking at her. You didn't know what to think! Aunt Effie had said you were going to have someone to play with, but this sister only slept and no one would let you take her outdoors. After awhile you walked away. If this sister couldn't play, you weren't interested!

Spring had come, and with it more adventure! The iron gate swung back and forth, back and forth. Suddenly you were on the outside – alone. You put your fingers in the holes in the fence and followed the patterns of the leaves and vines. It was fascinating how one started where the other left off. You began to race along with it until suddenly there was another gate and another walk and another porch.

The couch was comfortable and you sat down swinging your new shoes. No one came, so you daydreamed and finally went off to sleep. Suddenly someone was hugging you tight. It was Momma, who was saying to Auntie Peart, "But she never did this before!" "She's getting a bit older," said Auntie Peart. That's how you found out that beyond the iron fence and the bushes, the house had another, bigger porch.

The days went by. There were so many things to learn about, especially about what things were for and what you could do with them. There were emotional times too, when you had to find out what was right and what was wrong. Papa talked to you with love in his voice. You'd do anything for Papa quite readily. Momma talked with authority in her voice, making a *great* point of what to do or not to do. You felt inwardly defiant and resentful. Papa would say gently, "Do what Momma says." You'd do it. Sometimes you defied Momma for the pride in you couldn't let her *always* be right. Then you'd melt and say, "I'm sorry." She would say, "You don't love me." "Yes," you'd say in emphatic tones, "I do too," and then it was all over.

Now there were two of you. You with your golden hair and blue eyes and your sister with brown hair and brown eyes. You with your flashing smile and Helen with dimples which you envied a bit because they were talked about so much. Helen was walking now and you could show her the fountain and the birds and the leaves and vines in the fence.

One day, you took Helen up the stairs to Aunt Effie's room. Auntie Peart was standing at the bottom holding her breath. Aunt Effie was in bed. She had a visitor. They were talking so you listened while they watched you. The lady rose finally, saying, "Well, Effie, I must go. I'm so sorry you have to go to bed every month. Can't anything be done?" "Why do you have to go to bed, Aunt Effie, when it's not night?" you asked. Aunt Effie patted your head. "I hope you never have to," she said.

11

Another day, after coming down the stairs, you pushed on the portieres harder, and unresisting, they allowed you to fall into the forbidden parlor. There was a picture of a man on the marble topped table. He was smiling. Abashed at the happening, you asked, "Auntie Peart, who is the man in there?" Mystified, you led her to the picture.

"That was my husband," said Auntie Peart. "Where is he now?" you persisted. "He is dead," said Auntie Peart. "What is 'dead?'" you asked, unsatisfied. "God knows," said Auntie Peart, reverently. "Who is God?" you asked. This was the starting point of a major crisis in the family, though you didn't realize it until much later.

Papa and Momma had been talking about moving. With two children, Momma wanted to be off the second floor. Papa didn't know; he thought they couldn't afford it. On Plymouth Avenue, beyond the grocery store was a building with several "flats" in it. "Flats" was a new word. For a number of years, one had rented "living quarters," but not it was "flats" because the rooms were all on one floor. It was supposed to be more convenient and a bit "ultra."

Beyond the flats was a brick house placed right close to the main sidewalk. It was occupied but the people kept very much to themselves. The lot was wide. Behind the red brick in front was a large apple tree and further back a triple house, each section being a complete two-floor home. Papa didn't want to move there but Momma thought it would be much better as there was a fenced-in yard in the back for the children.

So, as when anything important happened, you and Helen stayed at Auntie Peart's until the excitement was over. It was a sad day for you, for now you couldn't go over to Auntie Peart's alone unless Momma took you and Helen, or when Helen was asleep. Many times you sat on the back porch looking into the yard wishing for someone to play with or something to do. Helen was three years younger. She was too little to follow your dreaming or perceive that in-and-out-of-this-world sensing of yours.

One day, The Little Girl came to play with you, who had come on many a bright occasion when the fountain, the stone birds and the iron fence had been your "alone world." You laughed and played with her in great glee until Momma looked out in amazement. Then The Little Girl went away so fast that you couldn't find her. At night, she often sat on your bed and played dolls with you until you fell asleep. She didn't live at your house, at #2 Plymouth Terrace, but often when you were alone and wanted her, she came. Sometimes Momma or Papa walked in and she went in a flash. You understood! She was a part of the "alone world." Sometimes Momma and Papa asked gently, "Who are you playing with?" "Emily!" you answered. "And, who is Emily?" they would ask. "A girl," you said.

Christmas came. #2 Plymouth Terrace had a fireplace and you children heard a great deal about Santa Claus coming down the chimney. Papa put some snow tracks coming out of the fireplace just under the stockings. Everyone rushed in. Your and Helen's eyes popped and Papa exclaimed, "Why look at Santa's tracks! He's been here." Momma, *she* rushed off to get the dustpan!

And then it was all over, all the fun of the presents. Helen went off to the kitchen and Papa went over to the drugstore and you were left alone. Emily [The Little Girl] came. She played with you and the new toys and dolls. She liked the new doll best and the carriage. After awhile, Papa came back to the house and he and Momma came into the room together. Emily forgot to go! Papa sat down in the big chair and you burst into uncontrolled sobbing seemingly without cause, but loving Papa found out between your gasps of breath that he had sat down on Emily.

"What's got into her, Frank?" said Momma. "I don't know," said Papa, "It seems almost too real for imagination!" And later you would catch them watching you when you played alone! Momma said maybe school would help, for it was going to be *the* fall before many months.

One day we went around to Peart's with Momma. Auntie Peart said, "Linda, why don't you come over more often." "I have too much to do and get too tired," said Momma. "I don't think I'm cut out for housework. I need something for my mind to chew on." You wondered about that but then you were too young.

Auntie Peart explained the recent happenings. A young man, Arthur Cooper, wanted to rent the unused side of the house. He designed and made ladies dresses. Auntie Pert said the large room would be excellent for sewing and he could use the entry by the big porch. You went around the house and looked in but he hadn't come as yet. Auntie Pert told Momma that she needed the income badly as it was getting more difficult to support her sister Effie. "Effie," she said, "would never be strong." You looked at pretty Aunt Effie, with her dainty clothes and sweet smelling perfume, and thought you'd like to be like her if you didn't have to stay in bed as much.

Today you were back swinging on the gate again and your heart was singing happily. Star Mosher came out the house across the road and eyed you questioningly. "Red head," he shouted, "Red head, you're nothing but a red head." Sobs overcame you and you ran to Auntie Peart. "Now see here," she said, "You go right back to that fence and tell him you're a red head herself!" And he was! *His* was bright brick red. You found that day that you could triumph without sobbing.

The fourth of July came. Papa told you it was dangerous but you thought you'd never forget! At five in the morning, the din began. It was almost frightening. No one passed with their horses that day. Cannonball firecrackers, sizzlers, dynamite caps, large firecrackers and small. All sorts of people had them, adults and children. Cans would blow up with tremendous bangs. Pranks were played. People got hurt but the noise and the confusion were wonderful! At night, a new variety arrived with sparklers, skyrockets and flowerpots, red lights and Roman candles. What an exciting world! People said it was because we were free.

Mr. Cooper came and you shyly met him while swinging on the Peart gate. He was coming around to the Peart side to see Aunt Effie. Aunt Effie seemed to be downstairs more now, sitting on the little porch near the fountain. Auntie Peart said it was because of Arthur. Momma said that Arthur was taking her thoughts away from herself. You knew in your young heart that they liked each other. The day came when Momma said that you were to be the flower girl and Helen the ring bearer at their wedding in the Peart house.

Arthur made two of the prettiest of pretty dresses for the two of you. Excitement ran high. Even Momma forgot to be tired and Papa brought over so much ice cream in a salted freezer that you wondered who was going to eat it. It was the first time you and Helen were ever really allowed in the forbidden parlor but today the gas lamps were lighted and turned up high and the room was decorated with such heaps of pretty flowers. There was a white strip on the floor to walk on and you were told to walk along the white streamers outlining it. Aunt Effie was so beautifully dressed that you made up your mind that some day you were going to be just like that and could hardly wait. Helen was so little she dropped the ring but you found it and everyone laughed gaily. Arthur hugged you both and told you that now he was your "Uncle" Arthur, and Effie Kelso was now Effie Cooper.

Grapevines covered the fence at the back of the triplex house. The children pulled away at the fence until there was a way thru. Later it became the way to school. You went thru to Dr. Woodruff's yard and down her roadway to Tremont Street. #3 School was just beyond. Dr. Woodruff knew Papa and Momma and said you meant a great deal to her for she was there WHEN. It was quite mysterious!

The first day of school you didn't go thru the fence, for Momma took you by the hand to the kindergarten, leaving Helen at the Peart's. Momma told Papa you seemed to suffer greatly for you were so self-conscious with the other children and scarcely could be made to stay. Later it was an old story, and home was so near you could run back to eat lunch and then back again, that is after you'd been going awhile. Once you ran back so quickly that you forgot to remove the apron Momma always insisted upon you wearing. You were so embarrassed because you'd cried – and cried some more.

The circular park was just up the street a ways. Papa took you there on many short walks but you weren't allowed to go alone. It seemed nice to walk with Papa. His hand was big and warm. The circular pool contained some fish. Flowers and a bench barred close proximity but Papa held you up to see their darting bodies. One could go round and round the pool many times.

Days followed days. Sometimes the dreamer, sometimes the tomboy, sometimes painfully shy, and next the leader and the showoff. One got so one couldn't guess the mood you'd get in. One day, you peeked into the principal's office and walked in and sat down and talked as if you'd known her all your life. Miss Echtenacker became fond of you. But sometimes you were off in the clouds so far removed in dreams that you noticed no one and were hard to understand. School work came easily to you. Sometimes the answers were known from study. Sometimes they seemed presented to you, though a second before they were unknown. Sometimes you knew what the teacher was going to say, but mostly it was study for you loved books from the beginning and were a fast reading beyond your age.

Then it was summer again, and the apples smelled wonderful on the tree in the front of the triplex. High into the apple tree you'd climb and sit there lost in thought. The flowers Momma had planted by the porch were in bloom. The sun shone brightly and the warmth made one drowsy. Papa wondered if a swing could be put on the tree and a new happiness was born. You could scarcely lift Helen on to the seat but once there you'd climb in and swing together until you were called. The days were glorious! Under the porch was a hole. You and Helen scooped it deeper with spoons until it became your cave. There were ant nests to watch, and hide-and-go-seek to play. Papa taught you "Up a Step" and tried to fool you as to which hand the stone was in.

The time came when you had to pick up your room on Saturdays. This meant to go over the floors, dust, and put it tidy. This always seemed such a nuisance but you found the quicker you did it well, the quicker you could go out again. So that was conquered too.

On one such Saturday, you heard such a racket coming down the street that you ran quickly to the front of the brick house. There, coming up Main Street, was the first automobile you'd ever seen. A man in a duster and a cap was steering the handle and a young lady sat with him enjoying the stares of the people. Horses reared on their hind feet, upsetting carriages. It proceeded about 15 miles per hour, for 25 was considered very dangerous then.

You told about the following experience long afterwards, for shyness did not allow the inner heart of you to be known. It was a lovely summer morning. You were alone. You were still quite young - six, I think. The dreamer in you cast it's shadow over you as you sat under the apple tree with its branches outstretched to the sky. Quietness flooded your being with deep peace. Something of life's meaning made itself known to you, child as you were.

The vastness of the universe and its oneness made itself felt. The floating clouds passed across the clear blue sky. Then you sensed that life had purpose in it and with the depth of a heart cry, raised your eyes to the blue above and gave answer to your mood. "I can take the hard things, God. I can stand them. I have courage." And then, carried out of the depths, you pondered upon the experience and wondered how it had come about. You never forgot that - nor that courage was expected of you. You were close to the angels then, but you didn't sense the coming life experiences.

Your bedroom on the second floor was opposite the bathroom. A window was contrived by a recessed section between the houses. This was your room. Many happy times of dreaming were spent in bed, thinking about the days happenings; Emily's unexpected appearances; your sister Helen's growing demands upon you for attention; the little quarrels and wrangles over dolls and carriages; and the doll house Papa had made for you two.

One night you were supposed to be asleep but were busy thinking. The bathroom door was open. The tin tub showed plainly in the gas light and the wooden frame around it was partly occupied by Papa. Papa was getting ready to take his bath. He had no idea that you were still awake at this hour and thru the open doors your bed was in shadow. Papa got all undressed and sat there to take off his socks. Shocked, you realized that Papa was different and that men were different from girls. You could not meet his eyes the next morning but he did not notice nor guess the turmoil in you. Papa had somehow changed.

About this time, the Mundy's who lived in #1 were to have a guest. Much talk had been overheard about the possibility of ghosts. Before this, your narrow limits of life had contained no fear except that of unexpected moments of shyness. Now you became afraid to be sent to the cellar for some of the preserves Momma had put up for the winter. You clung to the stairs, then raced around the furnace to the fruit cellar, grabbed the can and shot up the stairs out of breath. Could there be ghosts; white-robed creatures with slits for eyes? What were they? Why did they hold such terror? The reason for all that talk became apparent later.

The First Spiritualist Church had opened its doors in Rochester, and it was the first church of its kind almost anywhere. Furthermore, it was right there on Plymouth

Avenue. The papers were full of its doings and its thoughts. The Catholic Church near Plymouth Park denounced it and gathered its fold tighter around its people. The Protestant churches banned together in derision.

Momma forgot her housework. At last, her mind had something to get its teeth into. She was happier than in months. "Frank," she'd say, "let's look into this – it might explain Emily." Papa was not so sure but Momma was *so* happy. The Spiritualist Church overflowed with curiosity seekers expecting messages from departed ones. One heard of the Fox sisters thru the news articles by a Colonel Henry Olcott in New York City. Many pies didn't get baked. People met for "an evening" at friends and discussions were lively and forceful. Momma was in her element again and, after Papa came from the drugstore, the Mundy's and Tobey's spent evening after evening discussing this fascinating thought.

Momma eventually forgot Emily. At least, she found no explanation of her. Mediums became the topic. And now the Mundy's were to have a medium right in the house! All 280 pounds of Mrs. Moss arrived and were duly inspected. You were quite impressed when they told you she had to be helped in and out of the bathtub. You wondered who did it for her when she was all undressed. Not even Papa had seen you undressed. Momma always did that privately. "Little girls must learn to be modest," she had said. "It was protection." No one ever explained to you about Mrs. Moss and the bathtub, nor why it was so necessary to be modest.

Days went by and many bits of conversation were overheard and mulled over by you. "Mrs. Moss is a trumpet medium," you'd heard Papa say. Before the séance, there were knocks on the wall. Two knocks meant *no* and three *yes.* You heard about Indian guides and dainty dancing girls and trumpets floating around and holding hands in a circle. At last, you'd succeeded in getting Helen to sit quietly in the dark with you, holding hands in a circle. You tried it many times but no dancing girls came and nothing happened.

One day as you came up the steps, you heard Papa say, "Well, there must be something to it! Mrs. Moss certainly couldn't be those dancing girls. She can scarcely move. I *felt* that trumpet bump me on the head, and I grabbed that hand I saw ahead of me. It felt *real* all right, but it disappeared right while I was holding it." You entered the room and said, "Momma, I want to go to a séance." Momma replied, "No, but sometime I'll take you to the Spiritualist Church." Papa said no. Momma won out. But that was later.

That night, Papa came up the stairs to tuck you in and kiss you goodnight. He explained carefully that you and Helen were to go to sleep and that he and Momma would be right next door at the Mundy's. After he left, you whispered, "Helen, come over in my bed." You explained to Helen what you thought a séance was. "You ask me a question, Helen," and you answered her with two or three knocks on the side of the brass bed.

There were giggles and much fun. "Let's do it," you said. "Do what?" asked Helen. "Knock on the wall where they are." So you two crept down the stairway to the landing, to the place where the wall was common to the stairway and the living room next door. One-two, you knocked; then one-two-three; then repeating, getting hilarious with it until you and Helen were pounding the wall. Just then you heard Papa's steps and you raced up the stairs and into your beds, pretending to sleep. But Papa

22

didn't believe a word of it. Papa laughed and you laughed. "That's enough now," he said, "Go to sleep this time."

A frequent visitor to your Papa's store was a little woman whom Momma spoke of as being a spinster. The young woman discussed the subject of spiritualism on many an occasion with Papa. In the store were many labor and time-saving devices that he had contrived. One day, Papa put a chain under the counter and ran it to the front door where it was fastened. The little woman came to the store that afternoon to discuss the latest thing she had heard concerning "spirits." As she reached for the door handle, the door slowly opened wide with no visible assistance. "Oh! My God!" she screamed and turned and ran away as fast as she could.

One day, Papa came home from the drugstore. He had a clerk now. But Papa was different. Momma spotted it right away. "Frank," she said, "what *have* you done with your sideburns?" "Had them shaved off," said Papa, "Makes me look a little more dignified at the store. Everything is changing so rapidly now. The whole world has gone crazy what with motor cars, dead people talking, show girls doing the can-can, and now there are two fellow I heard about who think they can fly! Someone has to be dignified and carry on his profession."

"Not your mustache, Frank," said Momma. "No! Not now," said Papa, "Later perhaps." But it was much later.

During all this excitement, something did happen next door. The big house beyond the triplex on the way to the park was a beautiful place. Momma said you were not to go there for they could not keep up with the people. You didn't care much. The people sometimes patted your head, but you wondered what it was that Momma and Papa couldn't keep up with. Now the house was empty and a new family was moving in, and there standing before you was a boy, just a little taller, and his name, when you found out, was Rodney Williams.

Rodney piqued your interested. You were happy and gay when he was around. Helen no longer interested you. She was the *baby!* "You're a girl," he said, "and I don't like to play with girls." But day after day, the toe of his shoe was in the fence so he could look over at you; until one day, he walked around. Then the time flew by while you explored together; the swing, the cave, the ants' nest, the grapevine, the steps of the porches. Rodney brought over his wooden roller skates and skated around the brick house out front; out one sidewalk, across the main walk, and back again on the other side. It looked wonderful! "Papa! I want some roller skates," you said. He would respond, "But my little one, you're too little." "No, I'm not," you declared, "I want to beat Rodney." And so the roller skates were purchased, and hour after hour you practiced, radiant with happiness. It was so easy to make your heart sing.

The dray had driven up to #2 Plymouth Terrace. Out of its cavernous depths came The Piano. Many times you'd heard Momma say, "If only I had a piano." And here it was – a beautiful Steinway upright. "Oh! Frank!" said Momma. Papa beamed. He liked doing things for Momma. In awe, you crowded closer. "Don't touch it," said Papa, and that meant it was precious! Momma went running out of the room and came back with a box from the shelf where the music had been packed. Papa settled into a chair. You and sister sat on the floor. Momma played and played. You looked at her in awe and amazement. Momma, who was always so tired, was joyfully running her fingers over the keyboard! The piano sang. You slipped again into your mood of "aloneness." No longer were you in the room or with people. You'd vanished into the music and you throbbed and soared and laughed and danced with it. Your inner self seemed to reach on tiptoes to higher things.

You came to; still seated on the floor when Papa hugged and kissed Momma. "Linda, that was beautiful!" he said. "Oh, Frank, its been so long!" Papa hugged and kissed Momma again. She said quickly, "*Frank*, the children!" but she seemed so very happy. You'd never witnessed the depths of her emotion before. Suddenly you felt a kinship with Momma. Perhaps she *did* know how you felt sometimes, after all.

Momma had plans! She told Papa that *she* couldn't teach the girls. There must be a teacher so Grace and Helen could learn the piano. "Perhaps we could afford it," said Papa, "You know that chocolate sundae I worked on.

Well, it's beginning to bring in people from all over the city. They say it's the best in town," he added proudly.

So the teacher came and you two placed round lettered cardboard disks on the keys. You stretched your fingers up and down, learned scales and "exercises." At first you liked it, but then it got *so* monotonous. You sat, at times, attempting to make up tunes or, in gay fantasy, sweep your hands across the keyboard like Momma. It seemed as if, every time you saw Rodney waiting for you, Momma said, "Get your practicing done, Grace, RIGHT NOW! Time to play later." Later, Rodney would be gone and the whole afternoon was just wasted.

Finally, the teacher gave you a little piece to learn. "Memorize it," said the teacher. "Concentrate," said Momma. Over and over you went, but it was mechanical and uninteresting. The June recital approached. Uncle Arthur cut you and Helen pretty dresses. Aunt Effie sewed them and put bright ribbons in your hair. Momma got you your first patent leather shoes and long white stockings. "Don't they look beautiful," said Auntie Peart. Momma was anxious. She wanted you both to do so well. After all, she'd been a teacher herself in Erie, Pennsylvania, before she'd married Papa.

The day of the recital came. The smallest ones sat in the front of the room. There was a program and your names were on it. Helen walked up and took her turn. It was a tiny piece and she knew it well. The audience murmured and clapped. Helen was astonished at that and sat down suddenly. At last, it was your turn. You sat at the piano and started out bravely. Suddenly you stopped and started over. You did that three times, always stopping at the same place. The teacher fidgeted and reached in her music roll and placed the music before you on the stand. It was done. But it didn't carry you right out the window on a cloud like you'd daydreamed about so often; the piece sounded bangy and unrecognizable. You walked to your seat with downcast eyes and sobered face. You had come up against a solid world where concrete accomplishment mattered. You were bumped hard against external reality. You looked out around at the sea of faces as if you'd never really seen them before.

One day, Papa said, "Guess I'll buy a car." "Frank, whatever for?" said Momma, "You wont know how to drive it, Frank, and they are so dangerous." Papa said he'd learn, never fear. So the two-seater Olds arrived, splendid with dashboard, handle for steering, and kerosene lamps for lighting. The family all acquired linen dusters, caps, veils, and hats for riding. Papa said the car looked like a carriage but they had forgotten the horse. Sometimes it was hard to start and he would crank and crank and then with a bang it would go and Papa would jump in fast and start to steer. One day of fast driving, at 15 miles an hour, the car suddenly stopped on a railroad track. All of us could hear a train coming; the whistle was blowing not too far away. "Jump out quick," said Papa, "and push!" We did and just in time to clear the tracks.

There were days and days of roller-skating. You found yourself competing with boys, as by now there seemed to be no girls in the neighborhood. Around and around the fountain in Plymouth Park you'd go, skating faster and faster. One day you beat the boys around that circle,

27

especially Rodney. Triumphant, but abashed, the competition lost its fun.

Cornhill Methodist Church was around the corner and across from it the Catholic Church. The Cornhill Church was in the proximity of the back of #3 school. Now, years later, you remember little of either except that the church meant stiffly starched dresses for you and your sister and patent leather strapped pumps – the lasting style for little girls. The school was either two or three stories high with oiled wooden floors and worn stairways. One fact stands out clearly. You missed having Geography, for the school was then experimenting with new courses and in the change you never had any. Even today, it is hard to place countries and cities unless you've learned by reading or travel.

About your ninth birthday, you were asked by Rodney Williams' mother to attend the theater with Rodney. It was your first show and it was Maude Adams in *Peter Pan.* To this day, the memory of that occasion stands out clearly. Borne completely out of yourself in fascination and fantasy, you sat spellbound to the end, totally unconscious of the theater and the people around you and rose excitedly to answer, "Yes!!!" when Maude Adams asked the audience at the end, "Do *you* believe in fairies?

PART II

It is now 1966. I have recently received Margaret Turnbull's Echoes of the Past, *a brief history of the Town of Colchester and Downsville. That and daughter Janet's often-repeated request that I write out the stories that the Holmes 5 and I are often apt to refer to, has inspired me to begin. The Holmes and I often get really wound up while telling these true yarns and are full of laughter with their recall. So now I add the ones referring mostly to the summer seasons in Downsville and Walton. Perhaps I'll get back to the years in Rochester and later in Syracuse, if I don't get too busy.*

Well, here it is, Janet and Frank: Perhaps someday, your own children or your children's children may be interested in parts – especially family history and the flavor of the early 1900's and on.

Chapter 2

Thank you, Margaret, for getting me started to write the anecdotes relating to my younger years in Downsville. The writing of these stories and remembered happenings have long been asked of me, especially by my daughter, Janet Helen Lockwood (Paine) Wells.

Frankly, I won't know where to begin and it is hopeless to try to remember them chronologically. Perhaps some of Dr. Edward Holmes' children can give me help in this or even add events that skip my memory.

Two families, particularly, drew our family to Downsville in the summers. It was and is a small village in New York's Delaware County, in the Town of Colchester. In the early days, I heard the population spoken of as 250 people, and used to make the proud statement that 3/4 of the village was related to me somehow or other to the degree of 6th cousins. To say that I loved the place goes without question; for its peaceful beauty, nestled between the foothills of the Catskills, struck a responsive chord, the influence of which still exists.

It is a main street town with streets developing into roads leading away to Margaretsville, to East Branch, to Wilson Hollow, to Walton. There were a few notable places – some still in existence, but some now gone. Among them were the Old Mill that stood alongside of the brook that ran thru town and that once had a dam and a slight waterfall. There were Charles E. Hulbert's and William E. Holmes' Dry Goods Stores, the small post office near the brook bridge, Tub Mills Falls, and two churches, Methodist and Presbyterian. (No one seemed to care which one my cousins, my sister and I went to on Sundays, as long as we went.) There was the Paige Cemetery and an ancient one, two hotels, Downs and The Eagle, a pool room, a garage in "lower" town, and the now famed Downsville Covered Bridge – still standing and often pictured.

These were the days before the more recent dam covering twenty miles from Downsville to Margaretsville, an acquisition to help give New York City a larger water supply. It was also before a slightly larger population, changes in stores and in family names.

Downsville's Main Street curved thru the town from Tub Mill Falls, which poured over grey rocks in the spring and never failed to trickle down in the warmest summer, to the East Branch of the Delaware River and the Covered Bridge. The river flowed down some fifteen miles to the village of East Branch where it met the northward-turning West Branch. In the earlier years, many a logging raft went down the river, to be hauled to New York City or New Jersey by flat cars on the railroad. My grandfather, E. L. Holmes, used to tell of riding these rafts, holding the logs together with a pike. This traffic was finally absorbed by an acid factory built at Corbett.

Midway in the village, facing Main Street, and on a hill overshadowing the town, was Downs Grave. The village received its name from this early settler of the 1700's.

One of the early relative stories that my grandmother used to tell was of a family who moved to this area before there was any other nearby settlers. They had come from New England in a covered wagon, bringing provisions and a cow. A log cabin was raised and a garden planted by the two. There were eight children born during their years there, and then the husband died, leaving the woman and children many miles away from the nearest neighbor. Periodically, she had to swing the sacks of wheat over the horse's back and, locking the children in the house, proceed to the nearest grist mill thirty miles away to get the wheat ground into flour. On one such trip, the horse shied at a bear sleeping on the ground. She was unharmed but she never dared to lock the children in again.

The two previously mentioned families were those of my mother's parents, Mr. Ephraim L. Holmes and Mrs. Emmeline Dann Holmes, and sister Minnie Holmes; and brother Dr. Edward A. Holmes and wife May Hathaway Holmes and their five children, Marjorie, Mackay, Mildred, Joyce and Ephraim Paul.

The grandparents' house was in "upper" Downsville, on the Main Street beyond the C. E. Hulbert home, the Methodist Church, Dr. Brittain's house, a small building (the use no longer remembered), then a yard belonging to the family; back of which was Aunt Minnie's strawberry bed and a garden. Next were the Holmes' house, grandfather's law office, and an orchard of old apple trees (later to become the site of the old schoolhouse moved down the street from its former place). Back of the apple orchard was the barn and alongside of it the chicken yard.

The old orchard was a fascinating place for youngsters to play. It furnished trees to climb. Fenced in, it once contained great brutish hogs who also liked the apples that fell to the ground. I climbed those trees one summer day and went as far as I could toward the top. A branch broke and down I came to be investigated by those scary beasts. In answer to my vociferous protests, my mother exclaimed that I shouldn't be such a "tomboy."

When I was five or six, my mother, who could sew beautifully, felt that she could help Aunt May who had so much to do, if she made a dress for one of the girls. When finished, I was to take it to Aunt May. All but the buttonholes were ready. They had not been sewed. When I was back again, Mother asked me, "Did Aunt May like the dress?" I answered, "She liked the dress very much, but she was sorry that you didn't finish the buttonholes." My mother was very indignant and felt that Aunt May was not very grateful. She took it up with her. Now it was Aunt May's turn to be indignant. "I said no such thing!" she said. Mother came back to grandmother's and I was soundly spanked for not telling the truth. After the fuss was over, I was still feeling quite abused. "But Mama, I DIDN'T say she SAID it. She thought it and I KNEW it."

For a long time, I was an enigma to my mother. Papa said, "Linda, she sometimes reads people's minds – a kind of mental telepathy." I was grateful to Papa. He seemed to understand.

The chicken yard was a fascinating place to explore. The City of Rochester had no such creatures who liked to scratch gravel, nor had it a strawberry apple tree (the only one I seem to remember anywhere). We were not supposed to explore the woodhouse between the chicken yard and the house, but we often got in as far as our noses.

The cellar had a slanted outside door. We often stole down the stairs as quietly as possible. There was a large stone crock on the shelf. It contained Aunt Minnie's long remembered ginger cookies. We raided the jar often and thought we were getting away with it. *Years* later we found she knew all about it but was amused.

At butter making time, the old treadmill churn was walked by the dog Prince; the dasher in the butter barrel going up and down. We loved the taste of that fresh butter worked into pats and salted by our Aunt.

Aunt Minnie didn't like her name. Nor did she like the middle one which was Antoinette. Aunt Minnie would have liked her name to be Maude. She also would have liked curly hair. So Doctor Ed called her "fruzzel-headed Maude." In later years, we called her "Alph" which she liked much better, but that was after she came to Syracuse to live with my mother and father and me. When she came, the grandparents were gone, and the house sold. I felt badly when the law office, the house, and the orchard and the barn disappeared into other hands; but that's the way of things.

In the barn, the haylofts were fascinating. The wide beams we walked and jumped from into the hay and played hide-and-seek there. Outside the hay door looking down was the entrance for the cows and the manure piles of pungent odor. The horse stalls were below the door area. One day, while romping in the hay, I suddenly disappeared down the hay shaft into the horses' stall. The horse nuzzled around my feet and ankles. Never having conquered my fear of horses, I screamed and screamed until Lacey, the hired man, came running and backed the horse out. On another occasion, Lacey came to the rescue when the hay door in the loft flew open and I landed in the manure pile below. No cows around at this time.

Downstairs in the barn and under the shed were all kinds of farming equipment, wagons, and a cutter. A cutter was drawn by a horse. It had runners instead of wheels and was greatly needed on country roads in the winter. The cousins, sister and I played hide-and-seek in and out of the barn using all the equipment as hiding places. One day, in my fast moving endeavor to jump out of the cutter, I landed on the sharp end of a grass scythe and drove it into my leg. More shrieking! Grandmother and my Aunt tore up a good sheet to make a tourniquet until the doctor could arrive. That deep, round scar still exists above my knee.

Perhaps one of the earliest experiences was going after the cows. They were kept on the hill across the road from Tub Mill Falls. The cousins and we ducked under the fence and went down the rough field to the brook where we dallied to wade and throw stones. Then up the hill on the cow trails. It became steep after awhile but that was where we could pause to eat our fill of wintergreen leaves and berries. It always seemed as if at least one cow climbed up too far. Sometimes the dog went with us. Grandfather Holmes often wondered why it took us so long to drive the cows home but we loved the fun. I remember Tub Mill

Falls but that comes later with the coming of the 16th birthday.

Grandfather became stone deaf as he grew older. It was the reason he had to give up his law practice for which he had become quite well known. At first, we children were nonplussed as to how to communicate with him, but later took to writing notes. We children were great favorites of his. He used to pile us all in a one-seater buggy and drive us thru town. His death came when my sister, parents, and I were back in Rochester for the winter and school. I used to pretend he had just vanished. I had no realization of such events at that age.

The house seemed emptier with just Grandmother and Aunt Minnie. We ate in the big, roomy kitchen more often and saved the dining room with its red strawberry glasses and pitcher for Sundays. When it was cool, we ran thru the dining room from the kitchen to the "back parlor" as it was warmer there. The back parlor had a pot-bellied wood stove. It was wonderful to put your back or front to it and soak up the heat. In winter, the corners in the room were cold so all feet went close to the stove.

This back parlor was the scene of a story often told in the family. There was an aunt of great age, who had come to see Grandmother. She was a person who talked incessantly and with a staccato rhythm that was pronounced. Aunt Minnie was trying to read a book. The story became very fascinating and she became engrossed in spite of the background noise. Suddenly, the visiting aunt paused for breath. The silence was startling! Aunt Minnie looked up from her book and said, "What happened? Did the clock stop?"

I recall several anecdotes when I think of Uncle Ed. A country physician, he traveled many, many miles with horse and buggy or cutter thru the village and hills making house calls. (Who does this now a days?) On one occasion, I was invited to go with him. Uncle Ed was often silent with his problems and I rode along enjoying the views of the Delaware River and the winding roads. Suddenly, without warning, he said, "What kind of tree is that?" I looked but answered, "I don't know." Where upon, he muttered, "You city girls don't know much, do you?" The next winter, I studied trees back in the city. I wanted a better opinion of myself.

The Delaware River (East Branch) twisted and turned along thru the valleys and under the covered bridge. One fine day, Uncle Ed took my sister and me out in a boat. Suddenly, without warning, he pitched us into the water and yelled, "Swim to shore!" We were frightened for neither of us could swim as some of our cousins did by this time. With much frantic endeavor we made it to shore. We could swim after that and the river held many happy days for us all. It wasn't until a time later that I awoke to the fact that Uncle Ed was right there with the boat if really needed. At the time, it seemed mighty rough. Later, I lost one of my mother's best rings in that river, and how I hated to go home. I'd had special permission to wear it and never dreamed it would disappear while in the water.

The river holds other stories. Kay Holmes used to jump off the covered bridge. This scared me until he seemed to manage it repeatedly. I never even tried. It was too far down to the water.

One day Joyce Holmes, Mabel Turnbull, and my sister Helen Tobey and I went swimming. We were not in our accustomed spot, but nearer to the bridge. Suddenly, one of the girls (I don't remember which), found she couldn't touch the bottom with her feet. She became panic-stricken (she could swim) and affected the other two. I suddenly had to break the hold of the three and push them toward shore while shouting, "*Swim*! You *can*!" All made it but after it was all over I went limp on the grass; scared, when all were safe.

I loved the river road down to Corbett and beyond. The cousins and I walked down the way hunting berries and kicking our feet in the dust of the road. This was so much more beautiful than the city streets! Corbett and its acid factory and the loads of logs from the hills, seemed a storybook experience.

Over the covered bridge to the other side of the river was the very old cemetery where Aunt Minnie, Marjorie H., and I tried to make out the facing names on the leaning stones, and found some which recalled events to our minds. On down that side in East Branch direction was the farm once owned by Grandfather but that was before my memory.

In the other direction, in later years, the roads surrounding the coming Downsville Dam would be built which would change the general character of the whole area. Running off this road was a steep stony road climbing high to the Goetchius Farm (spelling escapes me). There were a number of young folks there. Joyce and I decided we'd walk up to see them and spend the day. We came to a woods fire part way up which was being fought by a number of men, but we kept going. The scenery back down the valley became more and more beautiful. Across the way, beyond a fence and quite a distance from the road, we saw a very attractive grassy knoll and started across to see the view from there. Halfway over, we heard a loud bellowing and the pounding of hoofs. We ran for our lives, made the fence, rolled under it and kept running up the hill until we suddenly realized that the fence had made us safe and then we sat down and laughed and laughed until we were weak from it. I do not remember the day at the house at all, nor the walk home, but the bull, I do.

Aunt Minnie used to tell of getting chased by a bull near Down's grave overlooking the town on Holmes Hill behind the Holmes Dry Goods Store.

These were the days of box socials. The girls brought a box of food enough for two and the boys bid on them. The girls were very careful not to let the boys know which one they had brought. The days of "dates" and "going steady" were not yet. Mildred H. and I got our boxes ready and carefully made them just alike with one inconspicuous distinguishing mark. We went to a house on the hills up Tub Mill Falls Road. There were many young folks there and all was very merry.

At last, it came time for the boxes of food and the bidding started. As my box was held up, to my astonished surprise, George Turnbull and Joe Rutherford started bidding against each other and kept it going – still higher and higher, until it looked like a fight was coming. Realizing it was my box, but wondering how they had determined that, I grew redder and redder until I felt like crowding into a corner. The boys reached $5.oo – an unbelievable amount in those days of infrequent cash. I felt terrible! Funny, I can't remember who really won, but I was so self-conscious and so unhappy I wanted to run. I couldn't believe they had been so reckless with their money. I didn't know either of them very well, but I was a city visitor and hence the attraction.

Twelve miles beyond Tub Mill Falls lay Walton, New York, over Bear Mountain Road. We had cousins over there too. These third cousins (the Arthur J. Holmes family) had a furniture and undertaking business. Kaveda used to help his father drive. One day, Kaveda appeared in Downsville driving an empty hearse. When he saw all seven of us in the yard, he stopped at Grandmother's house and visited for a few minutes. We all though the world of Kaveda and he was full of fun. Very shortly, all seven of us were inside that hearse and looking out the windows. We rode the length of the village scandalizing many of the upright people, I'm certain. Indulgent Aunt Minnie felt we'd gone too far that time.

On another occasion, I rode the streets of Downsville. This time I was on the bare back of a big, broad, gray horse. Kay threw me up on the horse. Kay liked to tease sometimes. He knew I gave horses a wide space, but he threw me up and spanked the horse's rump. We started at Grandmother's house; by the time the horse and I neared the covered bridge, I was shouting, "Whoa! Whoa!" to no avail. A man stopped the horse and took me off. Finally Kay came running. This episode ended in much laughter.

(Marne) Marjorie and I are about the same age. She and I thought of many diversions. In those days, you had to make your own fun. There were no radios, televisions, etc., no canned mechanical entertainment. Sometimes I think we were rather ingenious and I wonder if we really didn't have more fun and understand each other better than today's youngsters.

The coming of Ephraim Paul Holmes had us all excite and full of questions as to how such events could happen. We vied with each other for this care and wheeled him up and down Main Street. To this day, there is a picture of him bundled into a doll carriage. As he grew older, I do not remember that we were quite as anxious to keep track of him, except when it fitted the plans of the moment.

Then there were the days when we "young uns" liked to dress up. The attics contained discarded clothes, some older in style and some plain or decorated with beads and ribbons. Marne dressed up one day as an old lady, and I an old man. I elaborately affixed a mustache and got myself into trousers, and she into an old-fashioned gown. We imagined we could go thru town without being recognized, but beyond the bridge was the Pool Room. Some boys from there chased us across the street into the backyard of the Sprague's house. A high wire fence barred our escape and my borrowed trousers became impaled on the wire at the top. On another occasion, I wheeled Marne, or she me, the length of the town in a wheelbarrow, while dressed in what we considered sufficient disguise. While Linda, Minnie, and "Gram" carried on lengthy discussions in the big kitchen preparing food, stoking the wood stove or ironing with the "sad" iron, we cooked up many ideas - whimsical, fanciful and pleasantly mischievous.

One day, I rode off in the buggy with Uncle Ed. He was out to make his rounds as physician. The day was hot and sticky. The horse plodded on, stumbling occasionally on the stones in the road as he climbed or steeply descended the Downsville hills. Many houses were far apart but the barking dogs announced our coming and often folks ran out of the house to exchange greetings, the news of the day or to seek professional advice. Uncle Ed was well liked by all and *very* capable as a medical doctor. As we neared the top of the mountain across the river, Uncle Ed said to me, "Watch what happens at the next house." As we got closer, a woman with a shawl rushed out to the gate and began a whining tale of all "her miseries." Uncle Ed got out his black bag and produced some pink pills, which he handed to her and drove on. When out of sight and hearing, he burst into hearty laughter, which puzzled me until he explained, "There is nothing – absolutely nothing wrong with her except that she is lonely way up here. I've satisfied her for years with bread pills." Gradually, I came to realize that these medical excursions brought in little or no money to his own growing household. My own admiration grew as well.

Over the big kitchen and warmed by a stovepipe running thru it, was the bedroom where I slept in a spool bed. It smelled pungently of dried corn stored in a back room. Steep dark stairs led upwards out of the kitchen and from the passage between the kitchen and Grandmother's downstairs bedroom. I used to run up those stairs timorously as the dark seemed to hold mysterious things. Arriving in the bedroom breathlessly, I would close the door with the old-fashioned lift latch. The bed, the room seemed safe. Down the hallway toward the front of the house was the company room. It had a tall-to-the-ceiling-backed walnut bed. A beautiful old paneled bedstead and a high walnut cupboard to match. The bed now is in my

Grandson's house in Manlius, New York. The back was lowered years ago and usage has been rough upon it.

Aunt Minnie's room was next to the front guest room with its homemade quilts and bureau accessories. Its use was allowed only to my father and mother. My sister Helen was moved from one room to another so I can't place her permanently anywhere upstairs. The front stairway ran down into a spacious front hall with its mirrored coat rack. On Sundays, after church, we piled our coats and hats there and put on the designated play clothes. Aunt Minnie or my mother often played on the grand piano in the sedate front parlor. Both played, both were piano teachers. Aunt Minnie sang in church and on special occasions. I like to think of those days of happy freedom when the only tasks seemed to be to wipe the dishes, make your bed, go feed the chickens and gather the eggs or pick enough corn for dinner. The latter was a real task when we prided ourselves on eating six or seven ears apiece. Nothing tasted as delicious in the City of Rochester. Sundays brought chicken pie baked with chicken gravy and biscuits. Ginger cookies, corn and chicken pie are the only foods I particularly remember at Grandmother's.

Grandma Emmeline Dann Holmes was a slender, dark-brown haired, rather sober person, with years of hard work behind her; caring for a family of five children: Wayne, Marvin, Edward, Linda Belle and Minnie Antoinette, and in certain years, numerous hired help. When she died in her eighties, she still had her brown hair without signs of gray. Sometimes, I'm certain, we often annoyed her with our liveliness, but she never let us know. As I remember her, she was quite a "home body" and very rarely went away from her house or yard.

My sister and I were in Dr. Edward and Aunt May Hathaway Holmes' house down Main Street as much as we were at Grandmother's. To me, the house was the most beautiful in town with its parquet floors, its many-windowed rooms and the hominess of the whole. Aunt May was a spotless housekeeper. The house was always scrubbed and scrupulously tidy. Adding two children to her five must have brought a great deal of extra work to her. Of this, I had no inkling. Years later, I awoke to this fact when I had children of my own. Uncle Ed's doctor's office was part of the house on the upper side. On the opposite side was a long porch where we used to play, either there or in the yard or barn.

The five children were rosy, strong and healthy looking. However, Aunt May felt occasionally that they should receive a checkup by their father Doctor. Uncle Ed was extremely busy and had many "irons in the fire." After repeated attempts to bring the children to Uncle Ed's special attention, she hit upon a plan one day. All were dressed in their Sunday best, scrubbed and newly combed. All walked out the porch door and around the house and rang the office doorbell. "Here they are," said Aunt May to the surprised Uncle Ed, "ready for their health check." I can imagine Uncle Ed's booming laughter.

Beyond Aunt May's there was a house and beyond that the bandstand and the Downs Hotel (later the site of "The Concrete Block"). On Saturday nights, the village was full of people who had driven in every kind of horse-drawn vehicle. They came from miles around to hear the band concerts. My cousin Gus Holmes led the band for many years. The uniforms were distinctive and the music memorable. My cousin Charlie Holmes was also in the band and many friends and more distant relatives of the 3rd, 4th, 5th, and 6th cousin varieties.

One summer day, Aunt May planned a real ambitious musicale at her house. Folding chairs were secured and many people arrived in their best. The performers were the Doctor Ed and May Holmes children and the Tobey girls. All had been studying music. There were piano solos by Marjorie, Mildred, and Joyce; and violin selections by Mackay and Helen Tobey. The performers were up on the front stairs and were to proceed sedately to the parlor when their turn came. In trembling anticipation, I awaited my place on the program. I was to give some "readings" (characterizations), one of a little boy and a piece of pie. I had been studying dramatics in Rochester at the Rochester School of Dramatics. As the audience broke into laughter and applause, I ran back up the stairs to safety.

The summer days in Downsville were often long, lazy and sun-filled. If there was a heavy fog in the morning, it portended real hot weather. There was always swimming, reading, playing tennis or exploring the countryside. I particularly liked the meandering brooks. Speaking of brooks recalls another episode. Before the days of bathroom conveniences, a row of outhouses lined the edge of the creek that ran back of the homes on lower Main Street. The morning after Halloween found all of them tipped into the creek. This was greeted by howls of laughter by their owners. I think this involved Mackay and other boys. This was legitimate fun to the villagers. I sometimes wonder today if we haven't lost some of that sense of ready humor. A group of people good-naturedly returned the small buildings to their places.

One evening, Mildred and I were racking our brains for something to do. We came up with the idea of bean storming. We "borrowed" a bag of raw beans from Grandmother's kitchen and went up Creamery Street, diagonally opposite the house, and came to the home of our friends the Robinson girls, Belle and Grace. Their father was sitting in the living room in plain sight from the outside. We threw beans against the window and fled behind bushes. He came to the door, looked around and returned to reading. We tried again, and again he came to the door. Three times we did this, giggling the while, until we were afraid of the consequences. We came back thru the village, trying the same stunt at different houses and places of business, finally reaching the garage at the lower end of town near the covered bridge. Both of us were becoming faintly interested in boys as such. There were two or three young men inside working on cars. We threw beans at the window and ran around the side of the building. We attracted attention. On the third try, the side door opened and a gun was fired into the air. Thoroughly frightened, we ran in the dark and collided with a high fence in the back. Over the fence we went and fell to the ground. No more shots. A week later, the local Downsville News contained a query, "What two respectable young ladies recently climbed a fence and fell into a pig pen?"

As I sit here wondering what is next in this narrative, I suddenly recall a story of a former minister of the Downsville M. E. Church, a favorite of my mother and aunt. Back in the days of very poignant prayer meetings on Wednesday nights, prayer was held, followed by public confessions of sins and often conversations to better ways in life. On one such night, Sister Agatha (I'll call her by that name) rose and in a mournful tone and garrulously, went on and on about the many times she had not lived up to the expectations of Jesus and a Christian life. The account contained nothing startling except its long continuance.

Finally, she concluded in a dramatic voice that she felt so ashamed about all this that she felt like crawling under her bed at home and staying there. She sat down. Up arose a gentleman inspired by this long account and he also began a lengthy and mournful dissertation on his real and fancied transgressions and ended by saying, "I feel so ashamed of myself that I feel just like crawling under the bed with Sister Agatha!" The church was convulsed but tried hard to stifle it. The minister loved it.

I feel like saying at this point, "Just what did happen to the Downs Hotel and the bandstand. Did it burn or was it torn down?" I do not remember. Anyway, The Concrete Block arose in its place, backed financially by Mr. C. E. Hulbert and Dr. Ed Holmes. It contained the bank, a drug store, a movie theater, and down a few steps, a dance hall. The upper stories contained four - or was it six - apartments. Impressive fire escapes went up each side of the building, the first in town. Times were changing. There were a few more automobiles, the beginnings of many better roads, a few more people in town and a few more houses. The midtown Downsville Creek Dam had been leveled. There was a new Creek Bridge. Mr. Sprague, Kay's close friend, had moved down the river toward East Branch. Some folks had gone, remaining only in memory. Some had moved away. The Concrete Block seemed to mark a new era.

The Holmes and Tobey young folks were a little older. The fact that one of the village boys had begun to date a girl was both interesting and stirring. We found out that he was going to take her to the movies. Between us, we conceived a plan. We carried pails of water to the top of The Concrete Block, up the fire escapes. Leaning over the front roof edge, we excitedly awaited the coming of our friends. As they got directly under us, we tipped the pails. But the distance of the fall of the water allowed them to gain the safety of the hallway and the water fell *kerplunk* on the middle-aged couple following. Up came the manager with fire in his eyes and determination in his legs. By the time he reached the roof, we were safely down the other fire escape and away. We always wondered if he knew or guessed who we were.

Gus and wife Eva lived upstairs over the W. E. Holmes Dry Goods Store. They had three children: Frances (Peach), Bassett and another who died very young. Peach joined us in many of our activities. I regret I haven't seen her in years. Charlie Holmes had a son Charlie. Somehow he joined in with us infrequently.

One day, we were seated around the large table in Aunt May's dining room, five Holmes children and two Tobeys. Aunt May was in and out of the kitchen. Uncle Ed served each one of us the amount he felt we should eat. At times we were a little shy of Uncle Ed. He was a disciplinarian at the table. We were to be quiet. We were to clean our plates entirely. It didn't matter whether we liked things or not. They were there to be finished. No one dared to be finicky. On this particular day, Uncle Ed was exasperated and talked emphatically. Some one had taken a road worker machine and gotten it into The Concrete Block and down a few steps into the dance hall. There it was. No one could fathom how it had gotten into the place for the doorway was much too narrow and there was no logical way to remove it. Dr. Ed and several other men had worked all morning trying to! They had fussed and fumed, it seemed, at the effort. We all felt a bit scared and awed by the degree of his wrath. He didn't know what the village was coming to, when someone could perpetrate such carryings on. Suddenly he looked at all of us and then directly at Kay. I think we all trembled then.

"Kay," he boomed, "Did *you* have anything to do with this?" Kay answered in what seemed a subdued voice, "Yes." We felt for Kay – we hadn't known about his part in the event. We all expected drastic punishment to follow. Uncle Ed looked again at Kay. Then to our utter surprise, he leaned back in his chair and roared with laughter. The tension broke. "How did you do it!?" We were all laughing shortly, but I don't think anyone really found out how, though the doorway had to be dismantled and several people recruited to remove the machine.

One day, Uncle Ed asked us all to go salt a colt. The way to the pasture was six miles. The walk along the stony dirt roads was pleasant. The creek waters murmured, the sun shone thru the leaves of the trees. There were hills to climb. We were used to them. The Catskills were glorious. With the salting of the colt, we returned to Downsville, a total of twelve miles. When we returned, Marne said to me, "Let's play tennis." There was a new court behind The Concrete Block. We played several games before returning home.

That evening, there was the weekly dance in the hall. Of course we all went. Everyone for miles around went. There was no thought of pairing off on these occasions.

The girls were asked for individual dances. There were no programs to fill out in advance. If you were asked, all right. If not, you danced with another girl. No one gave it a thought. The dances were fun, exciting, exhilarating. Joyce and Mabel were sometimes partners with Helen. When coming to Downsville for the summer, I immediately taught my cousins the new steps current in Rochester. Sometimes there were grand marches, cake walks, round dances, do-si-dos. Always there was the waltz and the one step, and the square dance. We entered into the fun with exuberance and a surprising degree of vitality. My own love of dancing was tremendous. It could carry me away with enthusiasm. Mother knowing of all these activities – salting the cow, playing tennis, and dancing - in *one* day said, "I don't know how you can stand it."

Marne and I were searching our minds for something to do. We turned down many things in our minds but finally decided to sleep on the roof of Grandmother's front porch if Aunt Minnie would let us. Obliging Aunt Min said, "Yes, but don't disturb Grandmother about this. She would think it unladylike." So we gathered up blankets and pillows and laid them on the slanting shingles, anchoring them with Grandmother's "sad" irons. When it was darker, we climbed out the upper hall window and with many giggles we watched the town go by. We slept finely until the sun rose. Now we wondered how we'd get back into the house without being seen in our nighties. As we were maneuvering this, a farmer with a truckload of milk cans came along on his way to the creamery. He looked up and grinned. We dove under what was left of our improvised bed until the coast was clear again.

The tennis courts were moved to a plot of ground behind the post office. It became the place for picnics and games. To arrive there, one had to cross the creek on a wooden plank. Aunt Min loved to play tennis too. We were to meet her there. She arrived ahead of us. We met her, however, on our side of the creek. She seemed agitated. "What happened?" we exclaimed! Breathlessly, she answered, "There was a horse over there. As I arrived, it chased me. I lost my balance on the plank and nearly fell in." Her usual equanimity was considerably upset.

Across the street from Grandmother's, Theo Williams married Bill Baldwin. We knew them both. We were very interested. There were signs that we were growing up. On my 16th birthday, I gave a party at Tub Mill Falls. We strung the grounds with candle-lighted Jack-o-lanterns. I spent the whole day filling a new washtub with popcorn and making all kinds of goodies to eat. I had envisioned all kinds of games that were ready at hand and competitions in apple dunking and potato sack races, etc. I expected a truly outstanding affair – one to remember always. But instead, after eating, the young folks paired off and sat under the trees, stealing a quick kiss now and then. They were interested only in each other. I was disgusted. The whole affair seemed a total disappointment instead of fun.

When I was 17 years old, I had a throat operation in Rochester and because I was "run down" after it, I was sent out to Downsville for the rest of the winter. The cold weather fun of sliding down the hills, of snow fights, of building forts and tunnels, of skating on the river, of sleigh rides, of visiting my cousins' school, of learning how to cook under Aunt Min's tutelage, of maple sugar candy pulls, of just drinking in the snow scenes on the mountains, were a new Downsville. The first shy advances toward interest in boys began at this time. A young man from Corbett, Ray Woodin, gave me a quick kiss on Grandmother's porch after bringing me home from the Saturday night dance. I dreamed of him for days, but he occasion was not repeated. He moved out to Escanaba, Michigan, a short time later. Today when I see moving trucks with the name Woodin painted on them, I recall this.

One day, Marne and I were looking for excitement of some kind. It developed into the taking of one of Aunt May's sheets from her linen closet and proceeding up Gertrude Shaw's hill. The road winds at this point past the field where the new Downsville School now stands, and continues following the river down to East Branch. Gertrude was another of my distant relatives. We climbed the steep rocky hill thru the snow until we found a spot that could be seen from the whole village. There we anchored the sheet corners with large heavy stones and quietly went away, saying nothing about it to anyone. Spring was coming and with it the winter thaws. The sheet remained. One day, Aunt May sent us to the market near the brook bridge. We, Marne and I, awaited our turn. A farmer, with a pronounced drawl, said suddenly, "Waall, it is really getting to be spring. The snow is going off the mountains. But have you noticed that one patch on Shaw's hill? It doesn't melt." Marne and I were so choked with laughter that we had to run out of the store. Did we ever go after the sheet? Was it one of Aunt May's good ones? These questions came later.

During the winter I was in Downsville, Uncle Ed took me again on house calls in the cutter. The trees, especially the pines, were beautiful covered with snow. A big buffalo robe covered us. We climbed into the hills along the narrow roads, stopping at a number of widely spaced houses. While he was busy, I sat in the cutter and studied the valleys with the frozen river below. I wished I lived there. I loved it. The horse would move uneasily in its harness. The reins were thrown loosely over the dashboard. It was used to waiting. The afternoon was long and it began to dim. At last we started home. The snow in the fields was deep and windblown. Without warning, we turned off the road into them. Uncle Ed explained that it would be quicker to cross the fields. All went well until the cutter hit a big rock under the snow. Over the cutter I went and landed head first in the snowdrift with only my ankles and boots showing. I sputtered up to the surface to find Uncle Ed laughing uproariously. Mad and indignant, I sputtered, "Why didn't you help me?" He laughed out, "Couldn't! You looked too funny."

I loved games of all kinds and still do, as the grandchildren realize when they come to the house or camp. One such game was girl's basketball. The Downsville High School (the then new one, later to be replaced again) had a girl's team. I think it was either Marne or Mildred who was on the team, perhaps both. The team had basketball outfits that I quite admired for their attractiveness. One night a game was scheduled with an out of town village. The team lacked a player because of illness. After a consultation by my cousins with the principal, I was asked to fill in. I loved wearing the suit. Downsville won. I was as proud of that as the rest of them.

Then came the night of the big dance. Loving dancing, I put my whole heart and energies into it, and danced until late in the evening. By next morning, I had a high temperature and a very red chest, but so had a young man who was at the dance whom I didn't know except by sight and had not danced with nor been near as far as I could remember. Uncle Ed decided we had scarlet fever and quarantined us in. Within a day, I had whooping cough. Whooping cough at seventeen! I indignantly denied having scarlet fever. Uncle Ed was known for his fine ability as a diagnostician. He wasn't pleased with my vociferous protests. The quarantine continued. Aunt Minnie and Grandmother were put to it to entertain me. I found my own outlets in making several summer dresses for myself with Aunt Min's help in obtaining materials and patterns. I played her piano, read books and watched my friends out the windows as they went to the school and returned. Often they stopped to talk to me thru the glass. One spring morning, a beautiful little bunch of violets was stuck in the shutter. I found later that Joe Rutherford had placed them there. I was quite thrilled but it made me quite shy toward Joe. As I grew older, I wondered why I could be so very shy and self-conscious one minute and the life of the party the next.

One spring day, Mildred and I went to George Holmes' house near the mill and the brook bridge. We visited awhile and when the folks were called to the mill on business, we found ourselves alone in the house. Mildred and I decided we'd peek into the school principal's room as he lived there. Emboldened, we finally stepped inside. The house was still quiet. We turned down the covers on the bed and made what is called a short sheet that stops a person from stretching out full length. Then we got out of there fast and were innocently looking at magazines when the cousins returned from the mill. We got away with that one. Perhaps he figured it out. We never knew.

In the summer, it was decided that the Tobey and Holmes families would drive into Pennsylvania for a camping trip. We were equipped with tents, fishing gear, foods and besides all necessary articles, and Indian guide. The Indian guide was a friend of Uncle Ed's and was invited along to help us. The tents were erected and the camp laid out for use. All were to sleep on the ground on pine branches and blankets. All, except my mother. A wooden bench was constructed for her and it was plentifully covered with pine. We all pitched in to make her comfortable. Someone awoke in the night to see Linda sitting up in bed. "What are you doing, Linda?" was asked. "I am sitting up to rest!"

The Indian guide gave us names in his language. Mine was Ne-Ne-Ha-Gamma. When asked, he said it meant "the girl with the golden hair."

Our family did not stay in the camp too long. Soon, Mother said, "Frank, I think we had better go home. He is getting to interested in Grace. It is not safe for her." It might have been imagination on her part. Perhaps not. We returned to Downsville.

The time came when Uncle Ed was persuaded by Mackay to purchase a car. Many years of driving a horse had become a habit. The car was fine but it didn't stop when he yelled, "Whoa." I was told gleefully by Mackay that Uncle Ed didn't know what to do when a car approached him so he drove right over into the fields to get out of the way. Gradually he became accustomed to it, but I often thought he would have easily turned back to the slow jogging of the horse.

In these pages I have not forgotten that my sister Helen was there too. She was three years and two months younger than I and had younger companions. Joyce, Mabel Turnbull and Helen teamed up in many activities by themselves when not with us. Helen's middle name was Doris, which she liked better than the name Helen. We often called her that, so that as I write I feel divided between the two names but I did not wish to confuse anyone.

Pearl Walwrath, Mabel Crispell, Kattie Meinhold, Theo Williams, Jennie Hulbert, Nina Purdy, Eva Holmes, Maude Holmes, Emma Lindsley, John Holmes, and May Holmes were all friends of Aunt Minnie. Probably there are several others that I could add but at the moment they do not come to me. Several of these were related. And then there was a Mr. Conlon, a lawyer who loved Aunt Minnie. She refused him many times, sometimes on account of Grandmother, later on her own account. She never married. Perhaps she felt that marriage was not for her. Pearl Walwrath purchased Grandmother's house later on. Maude Holmes is still in Downsville.

Three names pop up in my mind: Archie Holmes, Esther Holmes, and Lucy Dann. All three were relatives. Only Esther is still living. Archie Holmes was blind. He was always cheerful and happy and loved us all. As children he often entertained us with stories. Maude Holmes is delighted to see us when we come to Downsville. The Dr. Holmes children often get there, as they now live in Middletown, New York, not too far away. Lucy Dann lived on a hill years ago, I think on the Walton Road or perhaps it was on Wilson Hollow Road. She lived alone high up on the mountainside. There is a story about her unusual pluck that I often heard from my mother. It was quite a distance from the village but she walked it at times. One day she climbed the apple tree on her place to gather apples for canning. The limb broke and she fell to the ground laying open her forehead over her eye. It was a wide and deep gash. There was no one to help so she threaded a needle and sewed it up herself and then walked to the village to the doctor.

There is another story that I remember when I think of the road to Walton. This is one of Grandmother Holmes' stories. Down Tub Mill Falls Road, perhaps a mile away, there were children whom Minnie and Linda liked to play with when they were young. They went there one summer day but were told to return home at a specified time. Engrossed in play, the girls failed to start and were very late getting home. Ordinarily, they would have been punished, but by being late they had missed the performance of a dancing bear. They were so disappointed, Grandma thought that was punishment enough.

I've referred to Walton over Bear Mountain Road. It was over this road in the late 1880's that my father Frank W. Tobey used to walk the twelve miles to see my mother, Linda Belle Holmes. Grandmother always put him up in the room with the throne bed. (I feel sorry that bed is so destroyed now; it signified my childhood so strongly.) On the throne bed were two light feather bed mattresses and a blanket. Grandmother didn't know it but my father hated feather bedding. He put them on the floor and managed to sleep without, carefully returning all in the morning – until Grandmother discovered it.

Linda finally went over to Walton to finish her schooling and to teach music. She and Lottie Hanford had many dates with the Tobey boys. Mother, upon graduation, went to Erie, Pennsylvania, to teach piano. My father still pursued her. Finally they were married in Walton, New York, and as my father had finished pharmaceutical school, they went to Rochester to live and to open a drugstore.

In Walton, my grandfather Clinton Charles Tobey was in the tanning business. I remember being admonished frequently to be trustworthy always as my grandfather who had gained the reputation of being so honest that "his word is as good as his bond." The Tobey house was one of the show places of the town. The house was very large, painted white, and had a large yard around it. It was very sturdily built as evidenced by the fact that it still stands, is occupied and is well over a hundred years old. Maria Barrows Tobey, my grandmother, outlived grandfather by many years. To me the place was an ancestral home. After Grandmother died, Emma Lillian, the only child who had not married, lived alone so my Aunt Carrie and newer Uncle Page Sinclair moved across town from their home to live in the Tobey house with Aunt Emma. It was 32 Townsend Street. The Sinclairs adopted a daughter, Helen Sinclair.

There are many memories of Walton also, its scenery, its winding river, the higher mountains, the steep roads down into the town, the sight of Bear Mountain Road rising to the top of the mountain on its way to Downsville, the Congregational Church, the roads which lead off to

Oneonta, to Unadilla, to Norwich. It was a larger town than my mother's. Here also were many relatives. Herbert and May, and their sons, Clinton and Dayton Tobey; Uncle Henry and Hattie and their children Anna (later Martin) and Martha (later Nutt); and Truman Tobey. My father had a twin brother Fred Tobey, who had gone to Sherburne to live. He and Aunt Ada had two children, Donald and Marjorie Tobey. There were also the Holmes' third cousins of whom I have already spoken. Arthur J. and wife had five children. They are all scattered now. Thelma married Professor Hargitt at Syracuse University. Last I knew they were in the south somewhere. Kaveda married twice. I thought he was in Oneonta but several letters to him have been returned. Doris married. Rex married and became a minister. Leitha married and continued to live in her old home for a number of years until her husband died. Also I had a "twin" so-called. She was Laura Marvin, born the same day, the same year and also had red hair though hers was darker. She was no relation.

The Tobey house had a large yard, pleasant with flowers, a summer house and a garden. We played innumerable games of croquet on the lawn and Ping Pong in the attic (before the house was rebuilt). In the barn were black walnuts and butternuts laid out to dry on the floor of the second story with an old iron block and hammer to crack them. The barn was fragrant with their odor.

During strawberry time, the Tobey Sunday morning breakfast consisted only of a huge two-layer strawberry shortcake lavishly covered with luscious berries and real whipped cream, together with coffee or milk. That was the entire breakfast. Grandmother said it was a custom handed down from her New England ancestors (from Munson, Massachusetts).

In Walton, there was an island in the river that was Island Park. We often had picnics and family reunions there. I particularly enjoyed bowling in the outdoor alleys with my sister and cousins, Clinton and Dayton. Baseball was another sport in which the women joined the men in both Walton and Downsville.

In Grandmother's house were beautiful antiques and heirlooms, some of which I longed for as future belongings. They were all willed to Helen Sinclair and carted away, or sold when Aunt Carrie died. I never heard about the sale of the house and much of the contents until months later or I should have been there to purchase some. I'm sentimental about family things. Because they are *family* they have added an intangible value. Things are things, but association with people makes them prized possessions. Luckily, Aunt Carrie had given me a set of very old Haviland brought from England and later from New England to Walton. It is very early china, she told me, made before Haviland was quite as dainty and fragile as it became later. In the family there was also a set of later Haviland which Aunt Carrie and Aunt Emma used daily without a thought of its more recent value. This became Helen's. I also have one of the Tobey shelf clocks which was given to them by my father. The old Tobey house was a gold mine of precious things and also much that was old and worn out. Again as in Downsville, the back parlor was the sitting room and the front parlor the special room. Later on, Helen was married in the house to Thomas Hoade in a very pretty wedding. They live now in Emmitsburg, Maryland.

But I must not forget to tell the much told story of Fred and Frank, the Tobey twins, when they were little boys (in the 1870's) wearing their velvet suits trimmed with lace. One day, Fred kicked Frank or was it Frank kicked

Fred? Anyway, a howl went up. Grandmother was ready to punish one of them but when admonished, he said, "I didn't kick him – my foot just lifted up and hit him." Grandmother laughed so hard that no one got spanked.

Besides Henry, Herbert, Fred and Frank, Carrie, and Emma Lillian, there was another son Stephen who died as a baby. Of all these relatives, only Martha Nutt, Anna Marvin's son in the real estate business and possibly Leitha Holmes _____ (I do not know her married name) are living in Walton now.

On our way home from Downsville and Walton to Rochester, we often stopped in Sherburne to stay a few days with Fred and Ada. There are pleasant memories of Sherburne also, playing croquet with Mr. Botsford across the street, having tea with elderly ladies in beautiful old houses and picnics at Rexford Falls, a canyon park where we climbed steep trails alongside of the stream as it tumbled down the hill from the waterfall.

I think on the whole, the winter school months in Rochester were waiting periods to get back again to the Catskill Hills.

Chapter 3

It is time to turn back to Rochester and #2 Plymouth Terrace. The Mundy's continued to live at #3 and discussions of Spiritualism continued and how it might undermine the church. We children heard a great deal but absorbed mostly what we called the scary parts. I was finally taken to the Sunday meeting by my mother. I remember that I didn't like the idea of dead people talking or even sending messages. It was a childish reaction.

One day mother announced we were to have a roomer. He was to have the front bedroom, and we must not bother him. George Rich was a young man who played the trumpet. We used to sit on the stairs to listen. Often my mother accompanied him on the piano. I think that at the time he was taking courses not to far away at the Mechanical Institute in Rochester. He moved to Syracuse finally and, years later, I ran into him on a dock at Sandy Pond near Lake Ontario.

When I was about nine years old, we moved from Plymouth Terrace and about that time my father sold his

drugstore and became a salesman on the road for Blau and
Brickner Drug Firm. His drugstore had figured largely in
the younger years. I had often climbed the fountain stools
for one of Frank Tobey's then famous chocolate sodas. One
day, however, when still quite small, I was exploring
around and tested the cigar-end cutting machine. It cut off
the end of my finger. My father quickly washed the parts
and then clamped them together with a leather finger cap
and tied it down tightly. To the amazement of everyone, the
finger grew together again. The scar is still visible though
greatly shrunken.

We often went on picnics; to Charlotte, to Highland
Park to see the lilacs, to Irondequoit Bay, to Chimney
Bluffs; to Genesee Park descending to the Genesee River
by one of the numerous pathways. At that time, Rochester
was called the Garden City of New York for the numerous
flowers in yards and parks.

We moved to 61 Gregg Street, to the third floor of a six
family apartment house. There was enough room when we
arrived up the stairways and the view was out over the
rooftops to the Genesee River Bridge. The piano had to be
hauled up the outside of the building. Mother couldn't be
without her Steinway. There were three bedrooms and a
sleeping couch in an alcove off the living room. Helen and I
each had a room to ourselves. Mackay Holmes came to live
with us so that he could take violin lessons. The alcove was
his. While Kay was there, there was a great deal of music
with my mother to encourage everyone.

I don't recall my father working on violin making and
repair while we were at Plymouth Terrace. Working as a
traveling salesman, he was away a great deal and began to
develop an interest in antiques, furniture, glassware, and
ran across many violins, cellos, violas and double basses. He

learned to play them all and began to study the adjusting of bridges and posts to gain more excellent tone, and finally began to make violins. Much love, varnish, oil and pumice, and polish went into the wood to give a beautiful, velvety finish.

Helen was a natural violinist. Her fingers were longer than mine. Cecila Poler worked with us on the piano, and ultimately Helen became a pupil of the finest violin teacher in Rochester, Signore Roberto Barbieri. She had outstanding talent, he said. My fingers were too short for the cello but rather painful exercises were devised to stretch my reach. My left hand shows it to this day.

One thing I loved, however, *was* given a chance. My mimicry of children and people made the family feel that I should have elocution lessons, so I could give "readings." Readings, the acting out of prose or poetry or a bit of a play, was a very popular accomplishment. I took lessons of Miss Roberts, who came from Henrietta, New York, to the Dramatic School of Art in Rochester. This led to many performances and parts in plays.

We did not stay too long at Gregg Street. But before we left, I was thrilled to be chosen as lead in the West High School play *Silas Marner*. I was to be Nancy Lamenter and Milton Bond was to be the male lead. I had known Milton for some time. He was excellent in Shakespearean roles and I had given performances of Kate, the Shrew, with him. Finally, after drilling and drilling in our parts, the day of the dress rehearsal came. Our coach, Miss Ellis, was a thin little woman, very nervous and exacting. Between acts, the players had to run upstairs from the stage to change their costumes. After the first act, as I rushed down the stairs for the second act, I slipped on the steps and badly sprained my ankle. The young players were fearful that our coach would find out, so I was carried up and down the stairs by my friends. Somehow I managed to get thru the dress rehearsal. It was two miles to the High School from Gregg Street. Charlie McCray got me home and carried me up the two flights of stairs. By this time, my foot and ankle were badly swollen and painful. What was I to do? The next day was the night of the play! My mother put on a salt pack and we hoped for the best.

The excitement of the play the next night carried me thru the first two acts but in the third act, I grew white with pain and my voice and lines lost conviction. Much praise for the first two acts but many I knew wondered about the third. Our teacher coach was so disappointed! Milton Bond had faltered in his part because of my slump in voice and actions. The secret came out finally. The school paper thought I deserved extra fine praise for continuing thru to the end. But I regretted that I couldn't have managed better.

During this time period, six of the drama students at the Drama School of Arts gave several plays. I loved all the excitement of preparation. I lost myself completely in the parts and "came to" with a start when the applause came.

While Kay was at the house, Thanksgiving Day came. Mother purchased a large turkey and stuffed it. As refrigerators were not as common in those days, she put it on the windowsill in the bedroom and went on with the housework. Somehow, Kay went past the window and down went the turkey all three floors to the ground below.

Kay dashed down the stairs and rescued the poor smashed bird. Mother looked at it with dismay, but as money wasn't too overly plentiful, she washed it, cleaned it and re-sewed and reshaped, and Mr. Turkey went into the oven after all and no one but those involved knew the difference.

The Gregg Street apartment house was not built as the best of them are now. We got all the noise of the other people, the odors of cooking, the family arguments and the late parties. My mother said, "Frank, I just can't stand this anymore." So the house at 107 Frost Avenue was purchased. It was a single two-story, but the inside decorations were dark and unattractive and the first winter found it cold and drafty. My mother was so discouraged that I remember her pounding the edge of the coal stove in the kitchen with her fist and saying, "I just can't stand it." My father decided he'd have to put steam heat in the house. He worked one room at a time and at first I was asked to hold pipes but before the house was completed I was a real steam fitter with quite a bit of "know how."

I was twelve years old. At Frost Avenue one day, my neck on the right side swelled up and it was pronounced mumps. Two weeks went by and the neck was still swollen beyond the jawbone. I had no great discomfort and I could eat the things that patients were supposed to be unable to tolerate. I said one day emphatically that I did not have mumps and no one could make me believe it. After much discussion between my parents and Effie and Arthur Cooper, it was decided that I should be taken to a doctor. He called it swollen glands from clipped-off tonsils (but not removed). Infection had spread into the neck. We were to wait and keep track of things. Finally the day came. The news was broken to me. I was to go to a hospital. It seemed like an adventure. I sang and skipped and told everyone that I was going.

Aunt Effie was very much concerned. My mother was upset too. So Aunt Effie took me over to the hospital and stayed while I was made ready. When the stretcher came, I hopped out of bed in my very short shirt and gaily got on, not waiting for help. Then I waved to Aunt Effie. The family thought it was all too funny. I didn't think so much of it shortly, for when I came out of surgery there was a tube in my neck, my hair was cut short and my head completely bandaged so that only a bit of forehead, eyes, nose, and mouth showed. All the rest was wound round and round even my shoulders. With self-consciousness to the fore, I suffered thru nine months of bandaged appearance at school and play. Then it was decided that I must go back and have the tonsils and the glands removed.

Marie Rossney, now Mrs. Jack Walton, lived two doors away. We became fast friends. The Rossney's were Irish and full of fun. There was a brother Frank. My mother was in good spirits again. I remember how she used to chase us playfully around the house and in and out with a broom. We made a great lark of it. Across the street were the Wagner's. Caroline Wagner joined Marie and me in a great deal of young fun.

When my mother was a young woman in her late teens, she suddenly rebelled about going to the village's two churches. Grandmother pushed church strongly. Either of the two was acceptable. My mother was very intellectual.

The sermons in either were based on fundamentalist doctrine. God was a wrathful Being. You must watch your step in what you did or everlasting punishment, hell fire and brimstone awaited your demise. The ministers would wax oratorical, "The wages of sin is death!" One day, mother informed her family that she was not going to church again! The shocked surprise was evident. "Why! Linda?" "Because," she said, "God is a loving God. A loving God would not sentence anyone to *everlasting* punishment, hell fire, and brimstone." Nothing would make her go back.

Coincidentally, my father was going thru the same questioning as a Congregationalist in Walton. When they were married, they went the round of Rochester churches but couldn't seem to find their niche. In no sense was it atheistic or non-religious on their part; it was the result of deep soul searching. When Helen and I were in the family, they asked themselves, "Where will we send the girls? They should have religious training." And so it was that the four of us went to a different church nearly every Sunday, but Cornhill Methodist was nearby so most of the time it was there. "We'll let them choose for themselves when they are older," was the decision. And several years before I left Rochester, I joined the Westminster Presbyterian Church near the Powers Hotel, and remain a member of that church to this day.

On Frost Avenue, Marie asked me to attend the Catholic Church with her. Mother thought that was fine! So I went many times with Marie. As so much was in Latin, I didn't learn much, but I liked the colorful interior and the ritual.

With a mother a Methodist-Presbyterian; a father a Congregationalist; a first husband a Universalist; the second, a Baptist; a son an Episcopalian (after marriage);

and a daughter, a Methodist; I sometimes wonder what I am. But at least it's a real religious education!

As the back yard was fairly large, my father said we must have a garden and that Helen and I must choose spaces that were our own to grow vegetables and flowers, but *we* must do this work. It was my first attempt. My mother said one day, "Frank, couldn't we have some chickens?" So the yard was fenced off in part for the chickens. Fall came and Dad let the Rossneys, the Wagners, Helen and I help him build a chicken house. We had four hens and a rooster. When my father was away, Helen and I were to feed and water them. Mother was not to be bothered! I named the rooster Teddy. For some reason, he became belligerent and flew at the toes of our shoes when we entered with feed. We grew to aggravate him by poking him with a stick. Teddy became subject matter for themes in school.

I walked every day to West High School and back. We figured it to be two miles each way. There were no school buses to take one. One day it was very icy. A fellow student was walking behind me not too far away. Suddenly I fell ungracefully, my feet flying high. He came and helped me up. I said, "Thank you." Whereupon I fell down again in a somewhat similar fashion. When he stepped up to help again, I said, "I'm sorry, I didn't do it on purpose!" I think he was as shy as I for he walked ahead alone and I followed. These seemed to be the days of embarrassing episodes. West High School had two (or was it three) floors. It had iron railings on the stairs. As I came up the steps one day, with classes passing to other rooms and the halls filled with young folks, my underskirt dropped to the floor (we wore camisoles and petticoats). Quickly, I picked it up and dashed down the hall, red faced. And did I blush easily!

Miss Young was our Latin teacher. She was a teacher all loved. I never was too interested in Latin, but find it has really helped in word derivations and in translations of other languages. Miss Young was hunchbacked. In her the students knew they had a real friend. One day in cold winter, the pupil next to me whispered, "#3 School is on fire." Just then Miss Young called on me to recite. I started, stammered over the words, got red then white and sat down suddenly. Miss Young said, "Is there anything the matter, Miss Tobey?" I told her, "#3 School is on fire and my sister Helen is in it." "You may go," she said, "I'll fix it at the office. Go quickly."

I ran out of the room and all the two miles home. Helen was fine! All children had gotten out safely due to a fire drill performed just a few days before, and also due to a dream. Miss Echtenacher, the principal, had dreamt that the school was on fire and that she was desperately trying to get all to safety. So the next day (in winter) she explained to the children in assembly that she was going to have a fire drill and all must make it a matter of haste – no one must stop for books, coats and caps or even rubbers but proceed to designated exits; that she wanted to see how fast the school could be emptied. It was carried out. Within three or four days, the gongs sounded again. No one had been forewarned but all walked in line without outer clothes to the front doors and then outside. This time they realized it was real. People all down Tremont Street took in the youngsters until their parents came. All belongings were destroyed. The children on the upper floor met the flames in the stairwell and had to race across the auditorium to another stairway. Miss Echtenacher went back inside as she remembered a lame child in the third grade and went to see if he was out. The newspapers made a story of the dream and its accomplishment. The school, old, wooden, with well-oiled flooring and dry from heat, burned quickly and fiercely to the ground. No one was hurt.

One evening as I got on a streetcar to ride home from downtown where I had been to attend the Rochester Dramatic School, I became increasingly aware that a man was following me. Frost Avenue turned off of Plymouth and it was a very long, not well-lighted block to my home. The man kept turning around in his seat and smiling at me. I KNEW he'd get off when I did. I decided to tell the motorman. I walked to the front of the streetcar and told him that I was afraid. He told me to stay on to the end of the line and if the man hadn't gotten off by that time, he would see that he did. I went back to my seat. At the end of the line, the man was put off. "It beats me," said the motorman. I was taken back to Frost Avenue, very grateful.

One night, my dad was out on his route as a drug salesman. Mother, Helen, and I were in the house alone. Suddenly I was awake. I slept upstairs. Below, set back inward into the house, was a vine-covered porch. I heard noises on the porch and jumped out of bed and looked out the window. Thinking it might be a burglar, I decided to scare him away. I opened my window wide and let it down with a bang. The man departed. As he went under a street light, I saw him as a large man with out-standing ears. I went into my mother's room and told her. "Weren't you afraid?" she asked. "No! I just thought I'd scare him away!" The police asked me for a description. They recognized him. He was just out of prison having served time for entering houses where he knew the man of the house to be away, criminally attacking the wife and older children. My mother kept a baseball bat at the head of her bed after that but felt she wouldn't have had it in her to use it effectively if she had needed it.

I don't know whether it was this or something else but the Frost Avenue house was sold and we were back with the Mundy's again in a two flat house. This time it was downstairs on Kenwood Avenue nearer to West High school and but a few houses from Chili Avenue.

Helen was becoming more and more skilled on the violin. Barbieri was to say eventually, "Take her to New York City for concert stage study. I've taught her all I know!"

Miss Root, my Sunday school teacher, was very interested in my dramatic readings and she also knew Milton Bond. In the meantime, "the six of us" at Dramatic School gave a play called *Thank Goodness, The Table Is Spread.* It was uproariously funny. The lead part was a maid in the family. I was that maid. Fritz Bonehill was the butler. We were asked to repeat it, which we did at a packed church and two other places. In the audience at one of the performances was the manager of the Baker Theater in Rochester. He asked if we would repeat the play at his theater at an afternoon and evening performance. As the curtains opened I had a moment of utter fright as I saw that sea of faces. The theater was filled to the ceiling of two balconies. It hadn't occurred to me that West High School students would come to see me in the play. As the curtain lifted, the butler was kissing the maid. That opened the play with a bang, a roar and applause. At the evening performance I had found myself completely and raced thru it with a great deal of aplomb. We got extravagant reviews, partly no doubt to the fact that we were local people.

One day, very shortly after, the doorbell rang at Kenwood Avenue. The manager of the Baker Theater introduced himself and asked my father and mother if they would give their consent for me to play the young lead in a stock company appearing at his theater and later to go on the road. My mother emphatically said, "No! She is too young. She is only sixteen. She must finish high school." During all the talk, I had become wildly excited and now I was crushed! For awhile, I felt my mother was just awful and that my father didn't dare to oppose her. I have to confess that it was years and years before complete forgiveness set in. At an earlier time, I'd wanted to take ukulele lessons. The twangy music; the spell of Hawaii had enthralled me. Mother had said, "NO! Frank, not that! She must take the cello!" And now the stage opportunity was downed. I felt that I knew what I wanted to do with my life more than they did. I loved them both, but I was miserable with longing. Stage struck, you'll say. Yes, probably! But the manager did not give up. He came the second time with a plan that would allow the finishing of high school as well. "She is going to college," said my mother. "What a waste of real talent," said the manager. But he didn't come again.

Wilbur Cross lived nearby on Chili Avenue. All the young people in the area played night hide-and-go-seek. It was great fun if not too dark. One night Wilbur caught me just inside a garage doorway. He hugged and kissed me. It was nearly a new experience. After that, I looked forward to its repetition. It never happened again. He'd gone shy and I was really disappointed.

My father found a cello - a real fine one. He found it in New England. It was marked Bergonzi inside. Cello lessons started. Painful exercises were devised to stretch my left hand. My hand would ache for days. At last I could keep up with the other three so we had chamber music ensembles. Mother played "her Steinway," Helen played her violin, my father played any one of the three instruments of viola, violin or double bass, and I played the cello. It really was fun. It was all classical music. I'm afraid I was more plebian then. I liked music with melodies, not what I called "dry stuff." This was a youthful reaction - one largely influenced by the love of dancing and a high school outlook. Dance music was not of my mother's choosing, though if I came home singing a new catchy tune, she would pick up the melody on the piano, improvise an accompaniment and we'd have a dandy tune. She had remarkable pitch. If I played a wrong note on the piano or cello, she would call from the next room, "That is B flat, not F."

The Mundy's upstairs were still interested in Spiritualism. They also loved our music. That was fortunate! Once, the Mundy's persuaded Mother and Dad to go to Lily Dale with them. They came back disappointed, saying the messages were inane, nothing really that a medium couldn't make up on the spur of the moment. There were discussions, even arguments, but it was then that their interest began to wane.

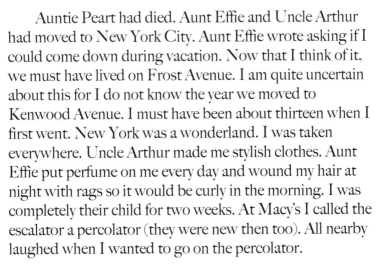

Auntie Peart had died. Aunt Effie and Uncle Arthur had moved to New York City. Aunt Effie wrote asking if I could come down during vacation. Now that I think of it, we must have lived on Frost Avenue. I am quite uncertain about this for I do not know the year we moved to Kenwood Avenue. I must have been about thirteen when I first went. New York was a wonderland. I was taken everywhere. Uncle Arthur made me stylish clothes. Aunt Effie put perfume on me every day and wound my hair at night with rags so it would be curly in the morning. I was completely their child for two weeks. At Macy's I called the escalator a percolator (they were new then too). All nearby laughed when I wanted to go on the percolator.

One of those days, Uncle Arthur brought home some material, transparent, lightly varied colored. He made a dress and under it a changeable colored taffeta slip and trimmed it with a light blue braid. Even I thought I was a walking dream. I'd never seen anything like it. We went out of New York to the Gramatan Hotel (was it in Connecticut?). It was a thrilling night for me and I knew I was attracting attention and found I liked it. At the time, Uncle Arthur had a job dressing the girls in the follies with his creations. Not that mine was not young, girlish and simply beautiful and suitable. One night I wore the dress to the front rows of the Metropolitan Theater to see the Rockettes. I was living in a dream world and wished I could stay with them forever.

But back to school again and home where everyone should amount to something and work hard for it or so it seemed. *My* next decision was that I was not going to college but I was going to become a nurse. I was beginning to feel a desire to be out on my own again. A gradual stiffening to parental influence was developing inwardly. Again the answer, "No, nursing as a profession is not good for girls!"

I had graduated from high school in 1914 and was taking extra courses as desired by my mother. So in 1915, I registered for college at Rochester University. But the first of September, my father had been hired by Hubbard Drug Company as a salesman, working out of Syracuse. Our household goods came slowly to us by canal boat and were unloaded near the present location of the park in front of the post office. They took two weeks to arrive. My father put us up in a rooming house on West Genesee Street as temporary quarters. I transferred my scholastic records from the University of Rochester to Syracuse University. We looked for a place to live, but even with four real estate men trying to locate us, only two flats could be found and nothing for sale. One was on the corner of Livingston and Stratford, but it wouldn't take the piano, so that was voted down. We moved into the only other one, at the corner of Ackerman and Stratford #902.

Our new home had angels painted on the ceiling of the living room and cornucopias of fruits in the dining room. Dad said perhaps we could paint them out and did.

I started college even before we were settled. Everything was so strange and so different. I knew no one! Conrad Becker was secured to teach Helen the violin. I took some cello lessons at Syracuse University carrying my cello across campus, often flung out away from me by the wind. I was settled into Liberal Arts, changed to The College of Dramatic Arts for six months but changed back again to Liberal Arts.

When at Drama School at Syracuse University, Lewis Palmeter was one of my teachers. As I liked readings based on children's dialogue, I was given a lengthy assignment. It was very humorous. I started to speak it to Professer Palmeter in his office a few days later. It was full of laughable passages. Suddenly I got a "catch" in my throat that had been very sensitive since the operation upon it. With one eye crying as a result and continuing the laughable childishness, I finally had to stop and Professor Palmeter and I were both overcome. It *was* ridiculous! He never forgot it.

I loved science and received a 95 in Freshman Chemistry. Now that brings me back again to a summer while still in Rochester. Harry Carpenter was my Chemistry teacher. He was an excellent one and made his classes love the subject. I did well in it. How well, I didn't realize until Mr. Carpenter came to Kenwood Avenue one day and explained something I hadn't heard of before. Each year, he and his wife took the three girl students who were at the top in grades in his Chemistry classes to Bass Lake, 70 miles inland from Brockport, Ontario, Canada. They had no children of their own and this was a great pleasure to them. I was one of the eligible students. Would my parents allow me to go for a six weeks vacation? I shouted with joy when I was allowed to. I found out that I loved the water when we crossed Lake Ontario in the lake boat. Then on by train to a wild, unsettled lake with just one camp - the Carpenter's. The scenery was beautiful and I thrilled to it as I had to Downsville views. The Carpenter's had a powerful motorboat and we went up the streams and into other lakes making portages at times. The lake shores were a tangle of fallen trees bleached white. The woods were hiding wild animals. I learned the names of many birds. The Carpenter's would crawl under some bushes and we with them and sit absolutely still without movement or talk for what seemed ages. Then the shy birds would come. I learned considerable about them and nests and the catching of big fish that summer. Also cheese might be added. That inland Canadian cheese was marvelous. Never have I been able to find any since.

It was at Bass Lake that I used to sit on a rock and daydream of Ray Woodin at Corbett who had taken me to Grandmother's from a dance in Downsville. It is now a good many years ago, possibly 1912 or 1913.

Having had Mr. Carpenter's excellent teaching, Chemistry I in college (then required) was not as difficult as it could have been, especially when forty pages of text was given for a class assignment. After the final exam, Dr. Brewer asked me to see him in his office. I could not guess what for! I went in almost fearfully. The self-conscious streak had not vanished! Dr. Brewer smiled and asked, "Did you think the exam was difficult?" "Yes, I did," I answered. "Did you have Chemistry in high school?" "Yes, I had an excellent teacher." There were other questions. Momentarily I thought, perhaps he thought I had cribbed. I felt indignant at that. There were about 100 students in the class, in a lecture room, each row of seats was higher than the last with the teacher's desk way below. There were only chair arms on the seats for writing. It would have been impossible to watch each student. But, I believe my answers and my manner assured him of my honesty. For he then said, "Only four people in the room passed that exam, Miss Tobey, you and three young men. I've had to flunk the rest. Your test paper was 95%." I resolved to write Mr. Carpenter and tell him.

One day near the beginning of the first term as I crossed campus, I ran into Connie Hutchinson. To my

surprise, she invited me to Delta Gamma where she lived. I
was pleased. I knew absolutely nothing about sororities and
didn't realize at first that I was being rushed. Eventually I
joined. Because I was nervous and timid with a bunch of
girls, when initiated, I got as far as repeating, "with this
fraternity," I ended up saying, "with this maternity" –
causing giggles.

On Ackerman Avenue, in the 800 block, Mary Louise
Light, a student at S. U. lived with her aunt and uncle, the
Ballway's. We got acquainted and often walked to and from
college. One day as we walked home we passed Sims Hall.
From out of the third floor sang a male voice, "Hello
Goldilocks!" After that, it happened repeatedly and many a
teasing and jocular remark issued from that window. We
eventually became acquainted with the young man. He was
Walter Roger Scott, "Scotty" to his friends, and proved to
be a cousin of an osteopath whom I was to meet later on,
one Dr. W. Kenneth Howes.

Mary Louise and I became close friends. She began
going with Ralph Montanna. One weekend, Ralph and
Mary Louise were going to a dance. Ralph said he'd fix it
up with a friend of his for a double date. The dance was to
be held in the dance hall over the drug store on the corner
of Colvin and S. Salina Street (now an undertaking school).
The "blind date" for me was Demetrius L. Lockwood,
"Dummy" to his friends. As I loved dancing, I had a
wonderful time. This started a round of dances,
entertainment, walking the trails in the woods, canoeing,
etc.

Dummy had a canoe at the Kaneenda Canoe Club at
the river end of Onondaga Lake. I learned to paddle and
the canoe was eventually named "uh-huh" after my way of
answering "yes." An extremely embarrassing incident took

place at the club one day. I was in the ladies outside toilet when my Delta Gamma pin dropped from my dress into the hole and could be seen below. The small wooden building had a low back opening. I hesitated about asking Dummy's help but finally did. I don't think he liked the job but the pin was retrieved.

On a rather cold December 4th, it had to be 1916, the six of us went swimming in the river in front of the Club House on a lark. I still remember that icy water!

In the summer of 1916, a bunch of Dummy's friends and their girls including Ray Hendrson, Sutton, the Henderson girl who later married Sutton (at the moment I do not recall the other names) loaded down with tents, equipment and with my mother as chaperone, paddled up the river, portaging at Baldwinsville and up the river to Phoenix. We obtained permission to camp on the edge of the river near an island. We had a wonderful week, with canoeing, exploring the area, swimming in the river, having campfires, and telling ghost stories in their flickering light. World War I had started in Europe in 1914. The young men were uneasy. How long before the U. S. would be in it and they would have to go. The camping trip was almost a last outing before what?????

Dummy and I had fallen "head over heels" in love – a fact disturbing to my mother as she wanted nothing to interfere with my education. He had graduated in June 1916 from Mechanical Engineering at Syracuse University and was about to take employment as a time-study man at the

Franklin Auto Works on Geddes Street. The following winter was a busy one. I had shifted to the School of Dramatic Arts at S. U. I now had to learn readings, stage directions, drama appreciation, etc. and always the dates with D. L. (Dummy) as frequently as we could find time, and often teaming up with Mary Louise and Monty.

The United States participation in the war was getting closer and closer. The young men grew anxious and restless. D. L. and I talked more frequently about getting married before he went IF he had to go. We consulted my mother and father. Mother was emphatic, "No! Let her finish her college. She is too young." Again I felt thwarted and unhappy. Deeply in love, I felt it more important than any education might ever be. Because of the often repeated *no*'s, D. L. and I decided we'd get married anyway. I felt strongly, I remember, that I had my life to live. I felt that I was old enough to make my own decisions.

We got the license and on February 4th, went to Dr. Frederick W. Betts' Universalist Church (D. L.'s) and were married. Mrs. Betts and a Mrs. Brown were witnesses. Then we notified our parents that we were on our way to Rochester in a "tin lizzie" D. L. had purchased. We had delivered a red satin box of chocolates to Delta Gamma and announced our surprise marriage. A nice little article came out in the paper.

We left Syracuse and went to the Seneca Hotel in Rochester. We were so very, very happy. I'd have a flicker of dismay at the thought that we'd have the devil to pay when we got home but it remained only a flicker. We were gaily happy with no thought of tomorrow but a little thought on whether we had money enough between us to get home again.

84

That night I had a very real and terrifying dream so much so that I screamed and screamed. As we lay in bed, Dummy with his back to me, I dreamt that a menacing black cloud came nearer and nearer as we lay there and finally settled between us pushing us apart. D. L. sat up in bed badly frightened. "What's the matter?" he asked. I had such a feeling that the dream was a warning that I didn't answer except to say it was a nightmare. I felt apprehensive, a feeling that diminished as time went on.

We were ideally happy in spite of the fact that I'd badly upset my mother who was having a hard time forgiving my young husband. I did not get back to college the rest of that term. We lived with my parents. D. L. started his job at Franklin's. We felt that as soon as we had a nest egg, we'd get our own apartment. In short order, I knew what I was expecting. Again the upsetting of the household for Mother now saw that there would be no further college for me. She turned to Helen Doris. She must finish high school and then go to New York City to study for the concert stage. BUT! What is that saying?

> *"All the plans of mice and men*
> *Sometimes come to naught."*

Is that it or am I wording it to fit my thought?

In April 1917, D. L. asked my permission to enlist. America was in the War. Great waves of patriotism were sweeping the country. Many of his friends were enlisting. With a heart that seemed to break within me, I granted what he so desperately wanted. "Perhaps your parents will think better of me if I do something for you, for them and for the United States," he said. I protested strongly, "They think a great deal of you. It is just that I disappointed them so badly in not finishing college." He enlisted.

Days and days followed as we expected the letter calling him into service. He loved the time-study work and I watched as many blueprints were prepared upon the kitchen table. He even reorganized the kitchen more efficiently, so as to save operational time, be more efficient and cause fewer steps. This amused me. Then he decided to teach me calculus. I didn't particularly take to it but it pleased him. That was enough for me!

D. L. had one piece he played on the piano. When or where he learned it, I do not know. It was *The Rosary*. He played it with delicacy and a depth of feeling that caused my mother to say, "He should have studied music!" He played it for me many, many times. It thrilled me deeply. My two memorized pieces at this time were Liszt's *Liebestraum* *(Song of Love)* and *Mighty Like a Rose*. We had our little musicals. My father lost himself in violin making and violin repair. Our flat had musical instruments everywhere. His working shop was set up in the kitchen or the cellar. Fortunately again, the Dr. Henry Neely Jones family downstairs enjoyed our music. Because of the war, we no longer thought in terms of a place of our own. Dummy bought a two-seater Ford with crank, snap-on side curtains and along the side, an acetylene tank to feed the lights. We took many trips out into the country, explored, had picnics and thoroughly enjoyed the times together.

My mother was to meet the next upset. Helen came home from school one day and said she couldn't get up on the stairs. She seemed exhausted. The family was thoroughly frightened. Dad and Mother took her to a doctor. It was discovered that she had exophthalmic goiter and her heart was affected. The advice of several doctors was sought. Medicine and rest were advised. The next several months Helen spent on the couch in the back parlor. We tried all kinds of activities with hands and mind to amuse her, but she was a real musician and longed for her "fiddle" and its music.

When summer came, Dad rented a cottage at Otisco Lake and the family went there to stay. It was across the lake from Amber and had to be reached by boat or by driving around and walking down the woods to the cottage. I stayed at the cottage to help my mother.

One day I decided to make some root beer. I followed directions faithfully and set it away on the kitchen shelves as directed. One day later, I heard a great noise in the kitchen. All the bottles had popped their corks and root beer was foaming out all over the kitchen. It took hours to clean up – to my disgust!

On one of the trips to the cottage from Syracuse on the road between Camillus and Marcellus, a heavy thunder shower came up. As we passed between the trees lining the road, a blot hit a barn not fifty feet from the car. The flash was tremendous and the crack of thunder terrifying. Our car stopped dead. For half an hour, it refused to go and then without apparent reason started again. The barn was shattered down one side but no fire resulted. It seemed a marvelous escape for us.

Helen did not seem to improve any even with rest in the quiet, woodsy surroundings near the lake. At that time, Dr. Wetherell was accorded the top goiter expert. He felt that it should be removed but the heart rapidity was a detriment. Helen was taken to a small hospital in Homer, New York, where she could have special care. She wrote pathetic little letters reporting all she could find out from the nurses. She seemed extremely lonely. Mother and Dad were frantic in their anxiety. We drove down there several times a week. Always she asked about her fiddle.

One day her heart rate was 144. Dr. Wetherell came to a decision. He broke the news gradually. It was a chance. It would be either an operation or perhaps less than six months. It would be a tremendous chance. Helen was moved to Cortland Hospital early in August. On August 5, she was operated upon. The anxiety, which had reached its heights in the family, seemed bad for me "in my condition" so the nurse insisted that I go to bed.

Exhausted by all the happenings, I went to sleep keyed very high. Before awakening, I had a dream vivid in details. I was with Helen. She was well, happy and very radiant. In the dream, I looked at the clock. It was four in the morning. I awoke and told my parents Helen would be fine again. She was to be happy and well. The night passed slowly. Four A.M. was looked forward to. By that time, Helen should be out of the effects of ether. At exactly four A.M.,

Helen died. I had misinterpreted, or had I? She would have been seventeen years old on November 15th.

My mother was inconsolable. Her world had crashed at her feet. I said it should have been me. Helen was the talented one. My father tried to comfort Mother but she walled herself in, seemed withdrawn and often unaware of us. I greatly felt the need of her but she didn't seem to notice.

Under the great strain of those days, early on September 18th, I began to have great pain. The doctor came. He said labor had started but must not be allowed to continue. It was too soon. He gave me some medicine. It did not stop the labor, but merely slowed proceedings. After two and a half days of labor, Janet Helen Lockwood arrived prematurely at 12:17 A.M. on September 20th.

Five days after her birth, D. L. came to the hospital to see us as he usually did after work. He reluctantly told me that he had kept the news from me but that he had to report for duty the next day and would go near Boston for training in the Engineering Corps. I was stunned but smiled bravely. "That's my girl," he said.

They kept me in the hospital for three weeks, partly because of Janet and partly because of what they called a difficult birth. I was in the old Memorial Hospital on West Genesee Street. Finally, I was allowed to go home. Dummy and I had named the little girl Janet because we liked the name. One day later, I found out that the Reverend Mrs. Janet L. Tucker thought we'd named her for her. I never disillusioned her. She was so pleased.

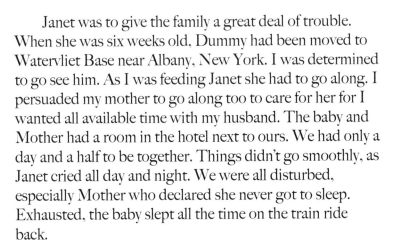

Janet was to give the family a great deal of trouble. When she was six weeks old, Dummy had been moved to Watervliet Base near Albany, New York. I was determined to go see him. As I was feeding Janet she had to go along. I persuaded my mother to go along too to care for her for I wanted all available time with my husband. The baby and Mother had a room in the hotel next to ours. We had only a day and a half to be together. Things didn't go smoothly, as Janet cried all day and night. We were all disturbed, especially Mother who declared she never got to sleep. Exhausted, the baby slept all the time on the train ride back.

The doctor found she had to be given a formula. She was hungry! But that didn't stop things. She continued to cry day and night. My father, mother and I took turns walking the floor with her and still she yelled. The only time she would quiet was when I wheeled her out in the carriage. And then I was to become accustomed to neighbors and friends peeking into the carriage and saying, "But where is the baby?" She looked so tiny in her blankets and oversized bonnet. I finally took her to a specialist. He said that her little stomach was not able to take the formula, so he weakened it and on every visit he weakened it again.

Finally, Mother, Dad and I were totally exhausted. My father suddenly said one night when we were trying to quiet Janet, "I wish you would throw all those damn clocks out of the window and give her something to eat." I doubt I'd ever heard my father say "damn" before and it impressed me. Next day Janet was bundled up. She was now nearly three months old and still tiny. She and I went to another doctor.

I said nothing about the specialist but handed him the formula proportions, told him she cried all the time and then waited. The nurse undressed her. She was looked over and tested from head to heels. Solemnly, he looked at me and said, "There is nothing wrong with this child except that you are starving her to death." He increased the formula and said to keep on increasing it gradually until she was having whole milk. "Feed her every time she yips," he said, "Follow no time schedule and let me see her in two weeks." In the two weeks, she was a smiling, happy baby. No more trouble. But oh, so hungry making up for lost time. Her hair was a darker red than mine. Dummy's black hair and my golden had produced a near auburn and our blue eyes another pair.

D. L. and I had a code. If a certain phrase appeared in a letter he thought things were moving out. When it came, I left for the next weekend. This time without Janet. Sunday night we slept in a downtown hotel. He was quite serious (the excitement of patriotism had sobered into a vague realization of things ahead). He wondered how I'd make out without him. He was very loving and solicitous. He had to be at his barracks at 5:30 A.M. on Monday. It was late before we slept.

Softly he patted m in the morning. I awoke. There he stood in his uniform all ready to leave. I sprang out of bed for his "Goodbye" with a big lump in my throat. He turned back and hugged me again. "I'll be thinking of you," he said, and the door closed. Suddenly, I knew. This was a real goodbye. Life would stretch ahead without him.

Overcome, I ran down the hotel corridors in my nightie and bare feet to catch him before the elevator came. The astonished elevator operator stopped at the floor to find us in close embrace. Then he was gone.

His ship sailed to France before Thanksgiving and weeks went by before I heard from him. Mail transportation was very slow.

Chapter 4

When Deme was at home, we had often gone to 261 Baker Avenue to see his father and mother. The name "Deme" is a new one, you see. It was given to him by my mother. The nickname "Dummy" had been acquired on a canoe trip with some of his friends. This was before I knew him. He had been quite silent all the trip and someone said, "Hey, Dummy!" and it stuck. Demetrius was a family name. It was the name of his uncle also, Uncle D. Van Schoick.

Mother Ida Rachel Van Schoick Lockwood was a short, jolly homebody and always delighted to see us. She had very heavy snow-white hair. I can remember the long talks getting acquainted and her creamed salt pork on mashed potatoes suppers. Mr. Luther S. Lockwood was of English descent. He was a very quiet person and seldom joined in the conversation. The Lockwood's had had four children but two girls had died with diphtheria. Deme's sister Jessie lived on Leon Street. She and Bruce Hunter had four boys: Dean, Earle, Robert, and Hugh. They are all married now with children and even grandchildren.

I loved to join in with this family. There was something of very solid worth about them. We had many dinners at Bruce and Jessie's. We also walked the six miles up to Uncle D. and Aunt Ernestine's farm high on Lafayette Road (when sold later, the farm became an abattoir - how awful!). Uncle D. and Aunt Ernestine were brother and sister. The Van Schoick parents had come to the U. S. from Holland. They were related to the Jerome's who lived in Pompey. The story of beautiful Jenny Jerome of Pompey who married into the Churchill family in England is well known. I used to twit Jan when she was older about her being related to the famed Churchill. "Oh! Mother!" she'd say. I had become acquainted with Charlie Jerome in my travels around the county. He lived in a house on the lot where the two roads came together in the village of Pompey. It had been torn down now and a new house replaces it.

As Janet was now over three months old and a happy child, one day my mother proposed that I go back to college and see how far I could get toward my degree before D. L. came back. I refused absolutely. "Who will take care of Janet?" was my question. "I will," was the answer, "If you will go!" So in January, I was back in Liberal Arts. But what a change in educational direction. Now it was all science - geology, astronomy, zoology, bacteriology, chemistry, physics, and botany. Professor Henry Neely Jones, head of the Bacteriology Department, lived downstairs in our house. I had Bacteriology with him and he proposed asking the University to allow me to assist him in his laboratories in exchanged for tuition. The University hired me on this basis plus $25 a month. Keeping up with my studies, assisting in the lab and hurrying home to care for Janet kept me very busy.

College was a very sober place during the war. The young men were largely gone and girls predominated. There was little social activity for most, and as for me, I was just too busy. One of my regrets stems from this: I really got little out of college life and developed few friendships. There was never any time besides the driving schedule. Each day I looked for letters from Deme. There were long waits and then I'd get several in one mail.

Janet's crib was in my room. I rigged up a light so I could read in bed and not awaken her and absorb those precious letters when the house was all quiet. One day, a letter said, "I'm in a plural adverb." There was strict censorship. It was a puzzling statement. I searched a map of France and decided it must be Nevers, near Chatteau Thierry. A great deal of heavy fighting was going on there at that time.

One day I was in Botany class. Professor Henry F. A. Meier was at his desk. I had a letter in my hand that I was trying to glance at and yet keep track of the classwork. Professor Meier was very understanding, "Read it, Mrs. Lockwood." I smiled my gratitude but shortly went very white. "Anything wrong?" I was asked. "Yes," I said, "He left a wooden building where he had been working with other engineers and walked a short distance. Within moments, the building was blown up by a shell and all his friends were killed. He was knocked flat."

I left my seat and went to a window and stared out at the campus. No one came near. The class proceeded but I

95

was not with them. After the students left, Professor Meier came over. "It's pretty rough for you, Grace," he said.

It was rough in other ways too. The Government allotment to me was $37.50 a month to care for a wife and child. The $25 a month from the University helped but during the summer I didn't have that. Dad and Mother felt I should learn to make finances meet now that I was married. They would furnish us a home and food. I was to manage the rest. But there were college books to buy, special foods for the baby, a bureau for her belongings, and too many incidentals. As for clothes, I had a jumper dress and a number of blouses and kept them going day after day until I was utterly sick of them. I didn't dare go to Delta Gamma for fear I'd have to pay something. Life became Jan and me, and little else. Waiting was difficult!

Added to the picture was the enveloping gloom that was growing around my mother. She mourned my sister deeply. I do not want to belabor these days but they were not easy. Often I dreaded to go home. The house seemed darkened. I found that my dad felt the same way. When he came home he would try to cheer Linda, and then depart to the cellar to his stringed instruments. There was no fun, no laughter, no music. The Steinway remained closed.

During a part of the time we lived on Ackerman, Marne came to live with us. I can remember her delight in trying to sleep on the porch swing on the second floor in the middle of winter covered with blankets like a polar bear, to awaken in the morning to find herself covered with snow. I wouldn't try it.

Always when Marne was around, Mother "perked" up. It was easier for everyone when there was an extra someone in the house.

One day my father received a notice that the place had been sold and that we were to move. Dad and Mother bought 741-743 Maryland Avenue, a three flat house. But a complicated situation developed. The Karcher's had to move into our flat a month before we could move out. The flat was dismantled and all packed ready to go and piled on one side. The Karcher's moved in, taking one-half of each room, and leaving their packed things on the opposite side. Everyone walked between. They took one bedroom and we still had two. Meals and cooking had to go in shifts. It was quite an experiment.

On Maryland Avenue, we took the middle flat and the other two were rented for $25 and $40 a month. Today, forty-nine years later, the same flats are $75 and $125 a month. How prices have crept up and up!

In the spring, we had a visitor – June Reed (Babcock), a concert violinist. My father previously had adjusted her violin for her. She wanted him to give it that glorious tone he'd managed before. She felt that the post had shifted or something had happened. She was fascinating to me. She had played for kings and queens in Europe, and had made a number of concert trips across the United States. She was full of gay spirits, talked music and philosophy and laughed and joked with my dad. I think my father confided in her, for she began to take steps to pull Linda out of herself. June got the Steinway open again and music back to our house. June made her fiddle laugh, cry and sing. I was thrilled. She brought a love of the finer classical music to me. She portrayed its richness. I couldn't get enough of it! My dad was happy! Fiddles and music had become his life. The trips on the road were necessary, but his work in the kitchen or the cellar on violins, violas, and double basses were more satisfying. The Post Standard discovered him and wrote a lengthy article with his picture taken in the kitchen surrounded by instruments and articles for their care, making and repair.

June finally said she just must go home to Billie, her husband in Wellsville, New York. Bill was also a musician. He gave voice lessons and was a concert singer. To me their marriage seemed quite bohemian. They came and went as they pleased when they had engagements. Either one took over the meals and house keeping when they were at home in their rooms in the Sutfin Block. I was fascinated with their easy camaraderie.

June loved baby Janet and often sat on the floor and played with her. "Will you make her a fiddler like me?" she asked of dad. June became a frequent visitor at our home after that. Sometimes she brought along one of her pupils and a violin to put in Dad's hands. I could not get enough of that blithe young spirit. I was tremendously happy when with her. Thru June, Dad and I flowed a perfect chord of understanding. All three vibrated to harmony, fun and light spirits with a deep substratum of emotional feeling about things. Arguments, flaring temper, and scoldings upset us inwardly and made us feel physically sick. The world could be such a beautiful place, if one would let it! Wars, aggression, mental depression, jawing were anathema.

Mother, June and Dad had many lively and deep discussions concerning philosophies and the meaning of life. Silently I drank them in. My mother always astonished me with her depth of insight and basic knowledge. June was always a delightful breeze that blew thru the house and cleared the atmosphere. Music dominated again. I was tremendously proud of my mother. She had an outstanding intellect. She was truly brilliant. Her music stirred the depths in me. Her true pitch amazed me. I couldn't strike a wrong note on the piano for she would call from the kitchen, "No! No! Grace, that is B flat or F," or whatever. A phrase of new music given to her by humming, she could turn into a production. She had great powers of concentration and memory. I thought her quite wonderful! But that negative side which could make her so "blue," so depressed, pleased me not a bit. She would say frequently, "You don't love me Grace." "I *certainly* do," I would answer, "But sometimes I don't love some of the things you do." And then I'd have to explain.

Marne Holmes came to live with us in order to attend college. I thought my parents were quite wonderful to give Marne and later Joyce a chance to attend. Mackay had had a turn with us for violin lessons. Mildred never came. She had had a major illness and her parents thought she'd better be close to them. Ephraim Paul went to Annapolis. At the time of this writing, he is a Vice Admiral in the Navy. He was with one of the ships at Pearl Harbor at the time of the bombing by the Japanese.

When Dad's vacation came, he felt we should go on a camping trip to Fourth Lake in the Adirondacks. Linda didn't like camping but the change would be good for her. On this occasion, or was it another, Marne was with us. When she was there, Dad, Marne and I climbed Bald Mountain, leaving Janet with my mother. "Climbing is just not for me," Mother would say.

Janet loved the arrival each day of the "Pickle Boat" which brought supplies. Janet was talking by now. My mother wished to be called MOM Tobey. She would not consent to being a grandmother. Janet's version of this was

"Todey," so my mother became "Todey" to everyone –
family, relatives, and even friends. I truly believe that Jan
came into the family sent at just the right time, for gradually
she took Helen's place in my mother's heart.

At last, November 1918 came. The world went wild.
The War was over! Whistles blew, bedlam and
pandemonium! The downtown streets were full of shouting
people, marching bands, milling crowds. I yelled myself
hoarse with the rest of them and couldn't talk for two days
afterwards. THE WAR WAS OVER! The Rochester
dream had not come true - Deme was safe! I became very
happy and gay. Soon! But the days and weeks passed and
still we were waiting for his return.

With nearly twelve months at the front in constant
danger from shells, D. L. had (as an engineer) charge of
examining damaged field pieces, artillery and all
implements of war, and ordering those that could be
repaired to the rear. It was hellish business and must have
seared his soul. The ugliness and horrors of war, I
deliberately blotted out of my mind. I just couldn't take it.
At times, it was brought close to me, especially when the
family got word from a buddy of Truman Tobey, one of my
favorite Tobey cousins, that Truman had been blown to
bits by a shell at the front. There was numbness in my heart
when I tried to comfort young friends when they had word
of the loss of sweethearts, fiancés, or husbands. My feelings
were constantly brought to the heights and to the depths.

Marne and I continued on with college. We even managed a dance or two, borrowing cousins, brothers or their friends for escorts. On one of these infrequent occasions, we danced until morning, mostly to the tune of "Margie." We had been to the University dance and came home to sandwiches and fruit juice and, turning on the Victrola, danced until dawn by turning the music way down to a whisper. Mother and Dad never said a word, perhaps they didn't hear us. The boys had to return to their out of town homes. Marne and I walked off to college. In the bacteriology laboratory preparing cultures for the students, I fell asleep. Professor Jones threw paper wads at me to awaken me. I explained.

Shortly after, an epidemic of influenza swept the United States, with disastrous results in many families. I had it twice. The second time it nearly finished me, but my dad also had the intuitive faculty. He awoke in the night feeling that something was not right about me. He walked down the hall to my room and rushed back to Linda. "She has a raging fever and is fighting for breath," he said. To get a doctor was an impossibility and the hospitals were already overcrowded. There were no "wonder" drugs as yet. Dad, with only his drug store knowledge of medicine, pulled me thru. He was with me every minute, staying home from business.

After I was up again, Dad went out and purchased a big porterhouse steak. When anyone was recovered from an illness, he got the steak. It was the only time he figured we could afford one. Prices had gone sky high during the war. Everything was higher priced, scarce or impossible to get. Eggs went from twelve cents a dozen to five cents apiece. Oranges, once a cent each, became seventy cents a dozen. "Don't get anymore, Frank," said Todey. Leather was scarce. If holes came in our shoes, we put in a piece of lining of some sort and continued to walk. Coal was hard to get and expensive. We took to living in the kitchen on the coldest days, scurrying thru the rest of the chilly house.

The boys in Europe were having a tough time too. Time dragged. It took time to wind up the details of the occupation. The ships, though full loaded, could not take everyone home at once. The waiting seemed tedious and frustrating. To some, the French girls were interesting episodes. D. L.'s letters spoke of this. He called it the moral breakdown of many previously decent young fellows. His letters sounded lonely and discontented. We kept on waiting. I wrote constantly and as cheerfully as possible. It couldn't be forever, I wrote. You'll be here before long, and we *will* have that little home of our own.

I had promised my mother to continue college only until D. L. arrived. Janet was getting cuter every day. She was late in walking but that came. I made her clothes when I could and was a very proud young mother with her chick.

Finally at the end of eighteen months separation, the wonderful letter came. It was written on shipboard, apparently coming across the ocean with him. "I'm coming home to you," he wrote, "It will take only a couple of days after I reach port." And then there was silence! Day followed day – no word, no inkling. Where can he be, I thought. At the end of the week, I telegraphed Washington. The answer came back two or three days later: "Pfc. Demetrius L. Lockwood discharged from the 28th Division. Should be home." I telegraphed the headquarters of the 28th Division and got the same answer. Now the days were worse than ever. When home, every outdoor sound caused me to run to the window to look down the street. I met the mailman at the door. No word!

At college, I mechanically went thru my classes and my work in the lab. The professors had gained knowledge of my predicament. They felt with me. One day I remember distinctly. Geology class was on the third floor in Lyman Hall. Professor Smith was detained. As he walked in the classroom, someone asked if I'd heard anything yet. I answered, "No," and trying to put on a brave front added, "but when he does get here, I'll certainly let him know *what.*" During this time, June came again for a few days.

Grandmother Holmes in Downsville was ill. She was 88 years old. Aunt Minnie thought my mother should come before it was too late. My father drove her and Janet down so Marne and I kept the house alone. Marne was and is a wonderful pal. She kept my spirits up.

One day I returned home before Marne and found a telegram awaiting me. It had been pushed under the door into the hallway. I opened it and sat down suddenly as I read it. Mrs. Albert Molyneau, who lived on the third floor upstairs, found me there as she came down to get her mail. I was speechless. No words would come. I handed her the telegram: "Pfc. Demetrius L. Lockwood seriously ill, Camp Upton Hospital. Probably won't survive. Come."

"You must go," she said. I responded, "I haven't any money. Dad isn't here." So Mrs. Molyneau gathered up what money she had and got further assistance from the neighbors. Marne came in. A train was leaving very shortly for New York City. I was rushed by taxi. As I left the house, I grabbed up Janet's picture and away I went.

Marne got word to Merritt Van Valkenburg in New York City and asked him to put me on the right train to Camp Upton. She got in touch with my father who was in Downsville and he came home bringing Linda and Janet. He contacted Mr. Lockwood, Deme's father, and they came to Camp Upton, arriving the following day.

Merritt took me to his apartment for there wasn't a train until evening. He tried to talk to me to ease the situation, but I was too dazed to know what he was saying. Merritt's mother came and she prepared warm food and also tried to help. It is pretty much a blank.

Merritt put me on the train. It was full of men in uniform just returned from France, now on their way back to the base after celebrating in New York. Many were drunk and all were boisterous. I was the only girl on the train. Their actions were rough, their language not what I was used to hearing. I crowded down into the corner of my seat next to the window. They draped themselves over my seat, ruffled my hair and tried to kiss me. As the train pounded its staccato on the rails, the talk grew more and more suggestive. I grew thoroughly frightened. An officer entered the car and took in the situation in a glance. All were ordered to their seats. The officer sat down beside me. He was a real person, a gentleman. He apologized for the boys; asked how I happened to be on the train; where was I going and why? "This is very irregular. Who sent the telegram?" he asked. I didn't know. He took me to the base hospital and checked the facts. He turned me over to a nurse and allowed me to stay.

The barracks were wooden buildings and stretched out so long that it seemed like two city blocks. They contained bed after bed the whole length, with soldiers ill with pneumonia. Deme had double pneumonia and flu, the nurse told me. As I walked down the corridor with her, she told me gently that he wouldn't live. "But he has to!" I answered. She had sent the telegram when she had realized. She had become especially interested because even in his delirium, he never swore or used obscene language as the majority of them did. He had kept calling for Grace. She looked up his history and found Grace was his wife. Against regulations, she telegraphed me upon her own responsibility. She might get called on the carpet. She didn't care. The war was over.

She let me sit by Deme's bed thru the night. She didn't think he'd come out of his coma. But I whispered to him repeatedly, "Dummy, speak to me. I'm here." And for about a half and hour, he did. He couldn't figure out how I'd gotten there. He knew I'd come. How was baby Janet? I showed him her picture. He couldn't believe she was his little girl. He had tried to imagine her. I kissed him again and again. I told him, "Get well and come home!" "I will," he answered, but slipped off into unconsciousness and didn't rouse.

The next day, May 21, 1919, just a half an hour before Deme died, my father and Mr. Lockwood arrived. He was unconscious. I hoped he could speak to his father. It didn't happen. "He's gone," said the nurse, "Come with me, Mrs. Lockwood." But all strength had gone out of me. I slid to the floor. "She can't" was the last thing I heard my father say. Dad told me later that I was taken into another room and a woman volunteer stayed with me all night. She had told my father that I talked as if to my husband and urged him to come home, saying that we must have the sons we'd planned on, brothers for Janet.

In the morning, we took the train home. My father and Mr. Lockwood made all the arrangements. The funeral was to be at the Lockwood home at 261 Baker Avenue. Dad phoned June Reed and asked her to come back. He thought she could help me. I felt I should be dressed in black. June wouldn't allow it, saying, "White is sometimes used on such occasions. You and Janet will be dressed in white."

Inwardly I rebelled about going to the funeral at all. Flowers kept coming to both houses, from friends, relatives, students in college and professors at S. U. One especially, I'll never forget. It was a blue dress suit, or garment box. I opened it. It was full to overflowing with wild violets from the woods. It was from my geology professor, Mr. Smith. The tears came then. I'd not cried before.

At Morningside Cemetery, as the service ended, my knees buckled under me again. June and Dad held me rigidly upright. I was grateful. I thought I'd never make it.

PART III

The days passed quickly. June took me in the woods and played to me there. The violin sang thru the trees. It seemed like a beautiful dream, one that I would hate to awaken from.

Chapter 5

It was exam time at the University. I just couldn't fall down in that. So I went and took them. It was difficult to concentrate. One paper I got halfway thru and then wrote, "I just can't," signed my name and left. Later, I tried to explain to him. My professor responded, "I never read your exam at all, Mrs. Lockwood. I gave you a 95% and tore up the paper and threw it in the wastebasket."

One day some errand took me to the University. Jan and I were dressed in our all whites, as we walked the corridors to Dr. Meier's office. "Why! Mrs. Lockwood," he greeted me. I felt his inward movement to put his arms around me – but he didn't. He talked to me awhile. He was one of my favorite professors. "Are you coming back next fall?" he asked. "My mother plans that I shall, she wants me to graduate." I couldn't have cared less.

June Reed Babcock went back to Wellsville. Soon a letter came asking if I could spend a couple of months with her. At Ma Babcock's farm off Hallsport Road, June had a cabin in the woods where she could write, read, and play her violin. "I'll talk to her with my fiddle," she wrote, "Frank, do let her come." Again my mother came forward to help me and offered also because of her increasing devotion to little Janet.

At Ma Babcock's lived Bill's brother Orlo, his wife Bessie and their little Junie, a baby. Orlo was an oil man. He shot oil wells in the neighborhood. In the Sutfin Block in Wellsville lived Lee Gonter and Joe Donovan was there a great deal, and of course Bill and June's rooms.

June's summer cabin was just what one would think of as belonging to an artist. Many pictures were on the walls. Copies of programs, pictures of famous persons she'd played for or with, pictures of European cities and the far west. I sat on a stool while her violin poured out her heart to me. I was deeply moved. Night after night we had our music. With her I was happy. Joe and Lee and June and I played croquet in the yard. We sometimes ran around in the high grass nearby in our bare feet. One day I stepped on a snake. My shoes stayed on after that. I was only 22. The love of fun was strong in me. Joe and Lee stirred up a lot of it.

Orlo invited me to shoot an oil well. The drill had been going deeper and deeper into the earth for days. He instructed me in the handling of the dynamite. I was to drop it straight down the hole and then run fast to a place a distance away before the oil, water and stones came up. The workers were standing around waiting. I dropped the stick and ran fast. Then I looked up and found I was the only one running. Orlo had played a joke on me to the amusement of the men.

At the studio in Wellsville, Bill had started giving me singing lessons. He said the voice was good but the breathing inadequate. Bill and June gave me many talks on their philosophy and how I could meet life. My consciousness expanded greatly under their tutelage. One day Bill said, "Sit down, Grace, and let's see what we can get from you." Placing a piece of paper on the table and a pencil loosely in his hand, he closed his eyes. Presently he began to write. This was taken from his notes:

> She has deep feelings, she can't always bring to the surface. She is very loving and affectionate. She must watch that, however, at times men misunderstand. At heart she is very straight-laced and very loyal to those she loves. This strength comes from the many tragic lessons she learned in Egypt as a dancing girl in the temples. Yes, she was of your group. You all have been together in another life. It is not strange that you are drawn together again.

There was more. I wish I had the original papers. It was my first experience with automatic writing. Bill had pages and pages of it written on other occasions. "Bill," I said, "What does it mean 'in another life?' Would that explain why as a child I frequently dreamed of a stone temple with high round pillars and many steps down to the sand? I would dance out of the temple down the steps and into the desert. It was all so very real." Now Bill was interested. He talked a long time about the meaning of life. That it was a school of experience. Thru experience we grew. Our lives on earth were as days in school. We had infinity in which to learn, but our goal was an opportunity and a lesson. If we didn't learn it the first time, it was presented in another way. Life was what *we* made it. We were the cause of the effects that came to us. I was deeply impressed and eager for more and more. The talks and the wonderful singing of June's violin began to ease the tension in me.

Back at the farm one day, I wandered away from the cabin and sat by a brook watching the water run over the stones. I yearned to live up to the best in me and never to falter. Deeply I prayed to conquer the recklessness I sometimes felt in myself, especially then. Physical need was strong, though I'd have been extremely ashamed to have had to admit it. Telepathically June got this too. I knew it when the conversation turned in this direction. "Work," she said, "Work your way thru. You will conquer." I was gone so long at the brook that the folks at the farm got worried and Orlo went out to look for me. The dam had broken. All the tears were being shed. I was bothered when Orlo found me. I didn't want anyone to know, but back at the house again, no one paid any attention. I think they were glad of the release.

The days passed quickly. June took me in the woods and played to me there. The violin sang thru the trees. It seemed like a beautiful dream, one that I would hate to awaken from.

One day June asked me, "I'm puzzled, Grace." Why do you never speak of Deme or of Janet?" "I can't speak of Deme," I said, "It breaks my heart. About Janet either, because she makes me think of him."

Finally the day came to go back to Syracuse to get ready for college again. Todey, Dad and Janet arrived in the car. She was sweet and plump. I gathered her up and showed her off to everyone. She was my little girl! I realized how much I'd missed her.

Back home again! Soon we had a visitor. Maurice Morris wrote us that he would like to come to our house for a few days. He was an English young man who had made his home in New Jersey. He had been a buddy of Deme's in the war and had heard so much of his wife and daughter. Maurice gave us many details we might never have known. He told us that Deme had been taken sick on shipboard before they reached the U. S. but that he had carefully concealed it because he was so desperately anxious to be discharged and on his way home to us. The troops that arrived were ordered to march up Fifth Avenue. It was rainy and damp cold. On return to the barracks the troopers were discharged. As this was in progress, Deme had collapsed. Maurice and others carried him to the base hospital. He heard later that he had died. He brought us a burlap bag of Deme's things that he had been holding for him. This was the reason why the War Department thought Deme had been discharged. The transfer to the hospital had not been recorded. Maurice wrote to me for several years. I answered his letters until one was returned marked "address unknown."

Duties took my attention. But soon, I began to be troubled about the question of death. What did it mean? Why were young people taken who hadn't lived out their lives? The question haunted me night and day. I wished I'd talked to Bill and June about this. What would they have said? What did the churches say? They surely must have the answers. During that fall, I made appointments to talk with every minister of every Protestant denomination in Syracuse and finally went to a Jewish rabbi and a Roman Catholic priest whom I'd met and liked very much, Father

McAvoy. Each talked with me, their own denominational slant influencing the answers. Not one satisfied me inwardly. Summing it all up, I thought what they said individually and collectively was, "If we were meant to know, we would have been told."

I longed more and more for my husband. There was little sleep at night. I dressed and walked out under the stars. I seemed nearer to him there. I got to walking to Morningside Cemetery, communing under the starry heavens. Answers tugged at me. Mother was afraid I'd be molested, but I was protected.

Marne came. College started. I found I could keep thoughts in check by work. I got acquainted with Florence Lockhart. Thru her influence, Mother and Dad encouraged me to go to Delta Gamma to live. Florence would be my roommate. Government insurance allowance was now $57.50 a month. Financially with help from my parents I could make it. But when there I felt keenly that I was an odd ball in that naïve company with their talk of campus boy friends, giggles, and dates. There seemed a subtle barrier between us. They seemed so young, so untried. There was only Florence who unconsciously had a bit of the wisdom of the ages within her. She has recently recalled the night when my stoicism broke and the heart allowed some of its sorrows to wash away.

At the end of seven months, I walked out and came back to Maryland Avenue to my parents, Janet and Marne. Belonging to Delta Gamma meant less than nothing to me after that. That first year back in college was grueling. Inwardly I had lost touch with education. I felt as if I were trying to reenter a world I'd known but that the *real me* was miles apart from the experience. I'll get thru this if it kills me, I thought. College work grew more difficult. I was now carrying a full schedule. I still worked in the laboratory, and Jan needed my company more. I had little time for personal thinking but still longed for the answer to the question of death.

One day I walked downtown alone and went upstairs in the Onondaga Hotel to the ladies room. As I left, I noticed that the ballroom was filled with people and a lecture was in progress. I stepped to the doorway and listened. Just as I did this, the speaker spoke of death and its meaning. I listened with growing excitement. I felt as if something had hit me squarely in the chest. I went in and sat down. I did not know whether I was welcome or not. This man had something to say that I *must* hear. I listened enthralled. I went up to the speaker afterward and told him briefly of my search for the answer to the question of death and how I'd found it in his words. I asked him concerning his knowledge and who sponsored his lecture. I had wandered into the lecture being given by L. W. Rogers, held by the Syracuse Lodge of the Theosophical Society. Theos meant God and Sophia, Wisdom; a study of God's Wisdom. The audience numbered over a thousand. Mr. Rogers gave me his book *Elements of Theosophy*. I read it all that night before I went to sleep. As I came to the chapter on reincarnation, I sat up in bed and exclaimed, "That's it. Of course it is! Bill and June know!"

The lecture and the book confirmed many of the things I had heard of in Wellsville. I knew of no source for the Babcock philosophy. I'm certain they had never heard of

Theosophy, but the source (The Ancient Teaching of The Mystery Schools) was the same, as I found out later. I joined the Society in January, 1920. I read the books every available moment. I really understood many things for the first time. This would help my mother, I thought. But for a time I couldn't get her to visit a meeting. Finally she did and joined readily. Her keen mind was busy again. My dad was slower but he and my aunt became members. Later my mother was president of the local Lodge for ten years and still later, I also, for ten years.

The Society was not a church. It was not a religion even, though often mistakenly called so. There was no dogma, no creed, no set ideas on any subject, not even reincarnation (a rebirth on earth in another human body). But it *was* a study of all religions, Divinely given earth, the philosophies of all ages, and the hidden powers in man. Several life times would be necessary to explore all its phases. The members I found to be of all faiths: Protestant, Catholic and Jewish and as it is an international organization, add Buddhism, Jainism, Mohammedanism, etc. etc. etc. It actively exists in at least 53 of the countries of the world except those now communistic. The studies are deep, satisfying, scientific, religious, spiritual and informative.

The study of Theosophy has led me into many avenues of thought. I value highly a sizeable library of books that I have acquired by purchase and inheritance, as a result of this interest. They include several versions of the Bible, the Bhagavadgita, the Koran, the Book of Mormon, the Book of the Dead from Egypt, the Tibetan Book of the Dead, books on the Ancient Wisdom, on psychism, E. S. P., archeology, mythology, and occult novels. There are also books from such leaders of thought as Socrates, Plato,

Herodotus, Emerson, Swedenborg, A. E., Kahlil Gibran, J. B. Rhine, William James, Meade, Le Plongeon, Churchward, Edgar Cayce, Hereward Carrington, Massey, etc. As well as Theosophical. These include Blavatsky's *Secret Doctrine*, many by Annie Besant, Geoffry Hodson, Ernest Wood, A.E. Powell, Clara Codd, L. W. Rogers, Charles Leadbeater, Sri Ram, Olcott, Sinnett, Krishnamurti, and others; also Manly P. Hall, Paul Brunton, Carl Jung, Ouspensky, Stewart Edward White, Eliphas Levi; others on the subjects of astrology, numerology, handwriting, palmistry, hypnotism: inspirational books by Claude Bragdon and others, books on Mysticism, Meditation, Yoga, on early Christianity, the Ancient Mystery Schools, the Gnostics, Hermeticists, the Dead Sea Scrolls, the Essenes, the Druids, Masonry; and by such people as Rider Haggard, Jess Stern, Ruth Montgomery, Sherwood Eddy, Max Heindel, Yoganand, etc. An avid reader, this library has been both a pride and a joy. Its perusal has covered years and years.

Let's go back to college days. Florence Lockhart was the one who interested me in Americanization. She had graduated having joined Delta Gamma in her junior year. She secured me as a teacher for a class of immigrants who were at Stearns Factory and needing to learn English. This brought in a little extra money, but the work was so fascinating that I would have gladly taught without remuneration. Florence had become the head of the county part of the Americanization League organized in 1917, by Mr. T. Aaron Levy. Its purpose was to help the foreign born to learn to speak, read and write English and learn about our government if they were interested in citizenship. There was also much paper work in the office besides the establishing of the classes in the county; assisting the foreign born with their problems; in helping relatives or family to come to the United States; in arranging programs to show the contributions being made to the States by the customs, music, dance and abilities of these people newer to us. Florence's work, as County Organizer, was in cooperation with the Immigration and Naturalization offices and with local and county educational systems. Individuals and industries were contacted as well. As time went on, in addition to college, I taught (in the evenings and on Saturday mornings) classes at the Onondaga County Sanatorium, Pleasant Beach, Marcellus, Camillus, Bear Road, Minoa, Skaneateles, Liverpool, and the Saturday class in Citizenship.

At college I now turned from Science to Sociology. As a field worker, Professor Almus Olver sent me out on casework as a student social worker. Thru this I discovered how some of the other half of folks lived. In some instances, I was appalled by the misery, the dirt, the immorality and the neglected children. I gave a talk on my findings to a group of high school students. They wished to help a family. Shortly all kinds of beautiful embroidered baby clothes, rompers, dresses and suits were gathered. Inwardly I was dismayed for I could see that some of these things would not be appreciated and would end up filthy and uncared for. I had indicated a family in Mattydale by the name of Charles and had given the students the children's ages. I had seen the filthy house, the slatternly mother. My first impulse was to change to another family in better shape but then decided that it was better to go ahead. The shock to the students would be beyond their experience and understanding.

I prepared the Charles family for our coming, feeling that perhaps there would be some little improvement. There was none. The high school students were disturbed and dismayed. They, in their comfortable homes, had never imagined anything like this. Going home, they asked many questions. I knew they would never forget it.

The field work practice so distressed me that I felt I did not wish to become a social worker as I would want to clean up every house, make it tidy, wash the children and comb them and give them decent surroundings. I *never could* see children abused or misunderstood.

When I graduated in June 1921, it was with a degree in Botany, and I could have had a degree in Sociology if I'd taken the time to write a thesis, then required. I never had much Botany but had taken all the Bacteriology offered but no degree was given in it then. Professor Jones wanted me to be a laboratory technician. He secured a scholarship in Boston for me where I could complete my preparation. At graduation, Mother and Dad were very proud of me. I had a Magna Cum Laude on the diploma and was wearing a Phi Beta Kappa Key. Little Janet walked in the procession outdoors wearing a Class of 1942 sign hung around her neck. The picture is around here somewhere.

Then came the time for me to choose between that scholarship and Janet. She was not yet four. I couldn't take her with me and I wouldn't go without her.

Marne was still in college as she had entered later than I. After I was the young widow, I was occasionally sought out for dates. Loving dancing and fun, I sometimes accepted. Sometimes Marne and I had double dates. I met a number of young men who were real fun and gentlemanly. I found I was also the hoped-for-prey of those who were not. I found out that I had grown up considerably.

One young man, who I could name, asked me frankly. I looked at him keenly, "What you need is to get married," I said, "but I'm not the girl." He never came to the house again.

Inwardly, my heart was still filled with longing for my husband, and the happy days when we were together.

Several years later, I met a young man mentioned on Fayette Street. He introduced me to his wife. Understanding flashed from eyes to eyes. But I *read* the two with that faculty which sometimes came spontaneously and could have said, "After the drive of the lower self recedes a little, when physical need is not quite as strong, you'll find nothing to go ahead on in your relationships. Life will become so arid between you, there will be separation, possibly divorce. Again, this is one of life's lessons – this one, to learn real soul satisfying love, and to know it as on another level than that of physical drive." One always wants so deeply to help but life's lessons can only be learned by the one involved. No other can.

In the summer, Marne had gone home to Downsville, when a letter came from June. A beautiful place by the bend of the creek had been found off the road from Hallsport to the Babcock farm. The bunch wanted to camp there for the summer. The bunch consisted of "Ma" and "Pa" Babcock, Lavandy in her 80's, Bill and June, Joe and Lee, John Cline and Villie, his wife. "Could Grace come? And Frank, could we borrow your Ford to use to get groceries in when needed?" By this time, June was so much a part of our family that I think Dad would not have hesitated if she'd asked for the moon. The camping was to last two months. Could he bring Grace down?

Dad wrote back that he would be on his trip but that he could manage to drive Grace as far as Horesheads, if someone would meet her. He could go on from there by train. Linda would care for Janet.

Joe was there to meet us. My father went into the drug store to get some cigars. I went to the car and sat down in the passenger seat. Joe said, "Aren't you going to drive?" "Aren't you?" I asked Joe. "I don't know how," said Joe. "Oh! My goodness, I don't know either! Don't tell Dad." So I jumped out. We insisted on walking with Dad to the depot which he didn't feel was necessary. The train left. I explained to Joe that I had had the wheel in my hands just three times and, as my father was scared about my learning, we had gone around one block only, each time.

"Come on, Joe, let's see if we can make it." Joe cranked the car and got in. We started off very slowly. If I'd had to back up, I wouldn't have had an idea as to what to do. We crept along until we reached Corning, New York. A parade was in progress. That was an obstacle I didn't dare tackle. We stopped until the parade was over and the road clear. Then we started again. It was a total of 100 miles to the camp where they waited for us.

After awhile, Joe said, "Teach me." But shortly Joe nearly ditched us trying to avoid a skunk. He gave the wheel back to me. Slowly, we crawled along. The acetylene lights had to be lit. Eleven hours later, we went up a hill and the car stopped. Now what! It couldn't be too much further to camp. We finally thought of an empty tank, and found a farmer who sold us some gasoline. We arrived at midnight. Then, of all the teasing and fun they had with us.

Twelve hours to come 100 miles! Where did you go? etc. etc. We had agreed to say nothing, so we kept still.

"Lizzie" was very temperamental. Standing outside at night, the car got cold and considerable cranking was necessary. One morning, when we needed supplies, the young men took turns, cranking and cranking by pulling a chain contrivance that Dad had rigged up. Still "Lizzie" didn't start. Exasperated one of them swore at the car and kicked the tire. "Lizzie" started. After that, Joe or Lee would swear first, then kick and then crank. "Lizzie" started every time. The boys said all she needed was authority!

John Cline, Lee, Joe and Pa Babcock had dug out the creek bend for a swimming hole. John had built a dance floor. Five tents had been set up with cot beds for everyone. There was a kitchen and an eating tent. Ma Babcock took over the kitchen. She was quite a talker and very much enjoyed by everyone, even when terrifically outspoken. No one took offense. "Ma was Ma." We swam, we danced, we had music with the fiddle and singing. June, John, and I wrote poetry. Pretty poor poetry as poetic form went, but the thoughts soared. There were many discussions around the fireplace reading and talking. Again, I head so much that I was reading in Theosophy. No, they hadn't heard of it. It was the ancient teachings they were referring to. I heard many things that explained my own personal psychic experiences. To them, it was all so natural a process, a sixth sense which was developing. The coming generation would show more and more of it.

John was writing up pages and pages of Bill's automatic writings. The law of duality was discussed in many of them, also called the law of opposites. Everything was positive or negative. Each thing had its opposite. Hot and cold, dark and light, good and evil. Sometimes the writings called it the law of choice. Man was given free will. Constantly he was given choices – brave or cowardly, happy or melancholy, harmonious or argumentative, loving or hateful, generous or niggardly, scolding or understanding, etc. Man made the choice and from the type of choice his life took direction. Every action affected everyone else around one for good or ill. One personally determined it. Each one had a tremendous responsibility! To me this sounded like the law of relationships of Martin Buber in *You and I* (I had studied this with Mabel Burlingham). There were other soaring thoughts as well.

One day the boys told of meeting five skunks on their way to the outhouse. I was timid about skunks. I didn't want to meet up with any. But one night, as I lay on my cot, there was a rustling in the leaves outside the tent walls next to my bed. I listened more intently. The movement of the leaves started and stopped and started again. Skunks! I crawled deeper into my blankets with one ear out to listen. Suddenly my fright grew. They were coming under the canvas into the tent just under my bed. I stiffened in alarm. Then a leap up on the foot of my bed. I yelled! Joe laughed. I grabbed his neck and held on for dear life. Joe was very apologetic. "I didn't mean to *really* scare you," he said. Villie with whom I was sharing the tent awakened. Our uproarious laughter awakened some of the others.

We all joined in to teach Lavandy to swim. She was 80 years old, but she made it. She was one of us. She said age didn't matter. It was the way you stood up to it that counted. Her spirit was just as young as ever. We knew it.

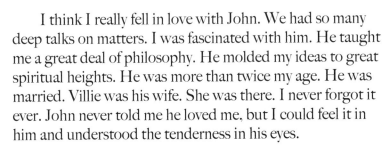

I think I really fell in love with John. We had so many deep talks on matters. I was fascinated with him. He taught me a great deal of philosophy. He molded my ideas to great spiritual heights. He was more than twice my age. He was married. Villie was his wife. She was there. I never forgot it ever. John never told me he loved me, but I could feel it in him and understood the tenderness in his eyes.

There was one camp episode perhaps I should leave out of his story, but here goes. Pa Babcock brought a big bottle of Virginia Dare to camp. After supper, glasses were passed around and I drank mine with the rest. It seemed very harmless and pleasant. I was not used to drinking. My mother and father abhorred it. Pa Babcock was up to mischief. He urged some more, I took it. John had gone on up to his tent. Bill said it was the priest in him, that he was disgusted! Suddenly I realized I was terrifically exhilarated and I left the group and went up to John's tent where he slept alone. Bill told the others not to go after me. "Let's see what she's really like, when her inhibitions are down." Villie, John's wife would not be held. She walked up to the tent and entered. I was standing just inside the doorway. What she heard was my plea for forgiveness for making such a fool of myself. She left and I went to June and put my head on her shoulder. I did not hear the last of it for many a day. June wrote a poem about "The day we Virginia Dared."

My love for John Cline was a precious thing. It ran deep and true. It was an added something to that love which I held for all of this group. They were all profoundly groping for the goal in life. They were searchers for truth, for beauty, for spiritual awareness. Artistic, fun loving,

harmonious, clean living, and clean thinking and yet
bohemian enough and non-conformist enough to at times
be totally misunderstood by some in the small village of
Wellsville. Their philosophy of life had an inspiring quality
which lifted me from a childlike acceptance of ideas into the
full bloom of adult thinking. But it was a gradual process
and not a sudden easy tuning of the mind. I can hear John
talking again. This I quote from some of his notes:

> The Self within one who is as yet at an early stage
> on the pathway to reality, is not asked to look at
> anything new but only to gaze with a *new and
> cleansed* vision on the ordinary intellectual images
> with which he has dwelt. This gazing with the inner
> eye opens the vistas to wider, deeper avenues of
> thinking. It becomes an exercise – a standing back
> from the whirl of earth and a viewing of the process
> of circling life. There is a universal behind every
> thought. A mind so trained transcends time and
> space and sees life always in eternal values. With the
> eyes of cosmic consciousness, he sees in
> relationships with others, the unity, not the
> separateness; in religion, he will go from the images
> and manmade dogmas and crystallizations to the
> mysteries of the Divinely created Self within. To rise
> to the heights is to literally pull ones self up by ones
> own bootstraps.

Two long summers of lofty thinking influenced my
whole life. I couldn't get John out of my mind. I worshipped
him. The years apart in age made no difference. He would
sit on a log with me at his feet. "Grace, I'm glad you're here.
Once you were afraid of me. It has to be resolved." "Afraid
of you," I asked, "Why?" I remembered no time when I'd
been afraid of him. "It was a number of lives ago," he

explained, "I was a priest in the temple. You were a vestal virgin. I desired you. It came to naught. Now we meet again on a higher level. There is nothing of the lower between us. We can soar as soul to soul. Everything on earth is basically electric and of opposite poles. The coming together of the two forces, negative and positive is the basis of creation. The sun does not heat the world. If you think of it, you know that beyond the earth's surface, it is extremely cold. The sun itself *may* be extremely cold. However, it has a positive force in its rays. Its rays activate the negative forces or rays in the inner earth. There is a flash of union. Earth's atmosphere is heated. Think of it, Grace! It may be 100 degrees in the valleys, yet the high mountains are in snow and they are nearer to the sun. 'As in Heaven, so Below' is the saying. The rays of the sun and earth create heat and this heat gives life to the things of earth. So the coming together of man and woman. The two, the positive and the negative are needed to create new life."

The days were long and discussions extended into the evening hours around the campfires. "We live in a three dimensional world," John would say, "When we leave it, the three become the fourth dimension. Because of the coming together there is unity. Time and space no longer are. Have you ever lost yourself for a moment in a swift and deeply satisfying experience which obliterated time and space. It was without mental command, uninvited, and rapidly slipped away again. Then once more you were imprisoned in your senses for the five *are* prison bars which keep you within the three dimensional circle. That moment of clearest insight, of eternal unity, was of the fourth dimension into which you also slip when the real you leaves behind its body-machine and becomes free in a less hampered world."

The choice of opposites in action was a repeated one with John. "Think of it, Grace. Can't you see them in everything? They are the determiners. The one you choose marks out your pathway. It is always thus. You are given a choice whether you are conscious of it or not. Sometimes the way stands out clearly, sometimes obscured and vague. The many World Teachers came to show mankind the Way to Live, the world of the Higher Self. Christ came into the body of Jesus for a short period of years. The message he came to give was essentially the same as the Teachers before Him, with a different emphasis. With Confucius, it was concrete wisdom; with Laotse, abstract wisdom; with the Teachers of Rome, law; of Greece, beauty, etc. etc. and with Buddha and the Christ, self sacrifice and love. We have yet to fully learn the latter. As the pendulum swings downward it returns upward. Always it swings a little further. Its stabilization is the unity I have spoken of. Man must know the depths and the heights thru life's school. The depths create conscience and character. The sorrows are often greater teachers than the joys. The saying cut over the face of the ancient temple "Know Thyself" is deeply profound. Looking upon life as an eternity of opportunity rather than the narrow concept of one life of experience only, changes the pattern of living remarkably. What we do not learn in one experiencing, is presented to us again. Earth's goal is self-mastery. No ability is ever lost. There is an eternity in which to develop."

June's message sang thru music, beauty and love of people. Bill's thru the development of character thru the study of himself and others. Joe and Lee were tremendously interested but helped us keep our feet on the ground thru their activity and fun. Ma Babcock was just Ma - lovable and outspoken.

I never felt I really knew what was stirring in Villie's reaction to things. She showed no jealousy of John's absorption in me, I truly think with their sense of the rightness of all things, she didn't even think of it. To the whole group, *the moment was the moment to live in.* It was brought to you by a destiny caused by your own self, thru time present and time with hoary age. Because you were you, that moment had a lesson in it somewhere. But I, being the youngest of them all in earth years, felt inadequate in the enormity of it.

And now it was time to go away, and I did reluctantly. Frank, my father, was coming for me. I had been driving all summer. I was the only one who could. Joe and I arrived at the station early and parked. Dad took the wheel and took us back to camp. When we were reading to leave for Syracuse, I playfully asked Dad if I could drive.

Then the whole story of Joe's and my twelve-hour drive came out. All were frightened at the thought. What if something had happened to us. But nothing had. Dad was unbelieving at first but shortly he understood. When I got home, I drove the car many times. This is my story of how I learned to drive by driving a hundred miles.

Marne was finishing her college. I was teaching English and Civics at the Onondaga Sanatorium in the daytime and had a class at night of 53 people in Pleasant Beach on Onondaga Lake. Lena Testi offered to help me. I could not have carried it alone with so many. I taught there for two years. There was a school trustee vs. the taxpayers fight about the use of the school which the taxpayers felt was built just for the children. This was not infrequent in the early days of adult education. I was assisting Florence Lockhart in the county program. I loved the work. It was a challenge. Florence was an excellent County Organizer. She was well liked by everyone. Mr. T. Aaron Levy often went with us on the trips into new school districts.

Florence's brother Gilbert was in Syracuse. She called him "Goo." I had a number of dates with Gilbert. I think perhaps she thought I might eventually become her sister-in-law. About this time Florence had met Silas Perry at a Grange meeting. It was a "go" from the start. Silas had come into the League office in the basement of the public library one day. When he left, one of the girls (I think it was Anna Marie Curtin) said, "That's the man Florence will marry." Silas and Florence, Gilbert and I got together many times. Once when Florence was driving with Silas in the front seat, and Gilbert and I in the back, being very weary, I fell asleep on Gilbert's shoulder, to the amusement of the couple in front. I got teased about this.

At home things were happier. Dad sometimes took Mother and Janet on his shorter trips. Mother was her second mother, her "Todey." As the days passed, Jan seemed to get cuter and cuter. I dressed her in the prettiest clothes I could find and put ribbons in her hair. I was tremendously proud of her.

Suddenly I head that Villie had died. Her death seemed so out of character with the group that I pondered it over and over and could not believe that she, with all she knew, could have taken her own life. But sometime later it was told to me that Villie had fallen deeply in love with a man whom circumstances prevented her from marrying and she had taken a way out. John understood but after that there were very arid years for him. Several years later, two lonely people found life together. Velma was sweet and dear, but John couldn't talk his heart and mind out with her. John had so much to give but Velma could not follow. One summer, I drove down to see them. This is also a number of years later. John and I had one of our rare talks. The woods were beautiful. Time stood still. We sat on the log at the campsite that had meant so much. John had needed someone to pour his thoughts out to. I listened raptly. Velma's special dinner nearly got burned. To us, it didn't matter. To her – catastrophe.

It was the last time I saw John. His letters continued but a telegram came within months that he had gone to that other world which he said one could enter so easily and so beautifully. "I will find you when you come, Grace." I had answered, "Perhaps."

Chapter 6

There is beginning to be a reluctance about writing so much about the personal *me*. To continue it, it seems as if *I* and *me* have to be separated and the *me* looked at as if by a stranger. Then I can write about this stranger, the *me*, as if I knew about her activities, reactions, thoughts, and emotions. This way I can look at the *me* with approval, or regret, but let life go on bringing its joys and sorrows, its accomplishments or its failures.

College had covered six years in time and effort, divided between it and responsibilities as assistant in the Bacteriology laboratory to help earn a living; the care of Janet; household duties and the teaching of night school. I really got to know few people very well, except perhaps the professors, those who were there between 1915 and 1921 in Liberal Arts and the School of Oratory. At times, I took a reduced schedule in order to take care of everything. The professors I remember the keenest were Henry F. A. Meier, Henry Neely Jones, Wm. Yerington, Dean Wm. Bray, Dr. Brewer, Dr. Hargitt, Dr. Raymond Piper, Lewis

Palmeter, Dr. Smallwood, Professor Smith of Geology, and Professor Katherine Sibley.

One thing was quite unique. I passed Gymnasium, which was required, by walking home at Miss Sibley's request, putting Janet in her carriage, and wheeling her to the gym. It seemed so out of character for Miss Sibley to take Janet and place her on a mat and play with her. Then she'd tell me it was time to take her back so I could make the next class. The walks were my gym. I think that I have written that marriage and college were not thought compatible at that time. I was unique in being the only married student – and with a child.

All the time there was an inner ache in my heart that often felt as if it would break its bounds. I loved having fun and activity with other people, and that avenue of release seemed nearly closed as well. My father tried to talk to me but I'd put such a tight little wall around the inner me that he could make no headway. Returning from Hallsport camp, near Wellsville in 1921, I took on more teaching work with the Americanization League. Florence Lockhart and I were together a great deal. Florence is one of those precious jewels one meets in life, genuine, whole hearted, a lover of people, having a keen sense of humor, a splendid executive and showed real pioneer spirit in organizing the county classes. We did a great deal together. In order to be with Janet as much as possible, I was at home in the daytime and taught night classes and a civics class on Saturday mornings. It wasn't very long before I was assisting her in the county work. Mr. Clarence L. Hewitt had the citywide program and there were day classes taught by Home Class Teachers, meeting in homes across the city and county.

The meeting of all nationalities and races was a tremendous experience. In the early days many of the people had not had the opportunity of going to school. To them, we had to teach writing, reading and the English language. This was done by direct method only. No translations were used. Direct method consists of acting, pantomime, the handling of objects and the naming of pictures of parts of the same. Names of objects were learned first, then action words, pronouns, phrases and then sentences. The lessons were daily needs in the home, in the store, with the children, etc. The teachers were instructed to make it a happy experience. Some of the foreign born already knew spoken English, some knew several languages.

There was frequent opposition to the use of the school building for these classes. We would work out a way to cause no increase in district cost but sometimes prejudice entered in. (I am so deeply gratified that this has very largely disappeared, forty years later.) I will give one example of the earlier problem. Near Bear Road District out North Syracuse way, there was a large area devoted to truck farming in the years around 1920. The farmers were non-citizen Italians. Their crops thrived with the constant care given them by all the members of the family. The American farms in the same area were noticeably run down and looked scrubby and unattractive. I always thought some envy existed in the picture. One of the immigrant farmers asked for a class. Mr. T. Aaron Levy, a well-known and beloved figure in Syracuse for a good many years, went with Florence and me to meet the school board at the school. We had figured out the total cost for the winter, had explained the program and told of other schools already in operation. He was a ready talker and presented it very well. A vote was taken by the school board and, to our dismay, it was voted down.

But not out. We asked the leader of the Italian group if any one had a large kitchen and would he find out if we could use it two days a week for two hours each. The class was continued in a farmhouse kitchen for two years. Then the Bear Road School Board asked us if the class could be moved to the schoolhouse. This is only one of several stories. I could write a book on Americanization League experiences but this account is already assuming proportions.

When Silas and Florence Parry became engaged, there was an announcement party at 741-743 Maryland Avenue. Florence asked me if I'd like to apply for her job for she was going home to get ready to be married. The County Committee of the League had the decision between another applicant and me. I got the decision. Florence was to leave the League the first of November 1922.

I came home one day in late spring 1922 and was thoroughly surprised by the announcement by my parents that I was to go to Europe for three months with Dr. Flick and his wife and a total of 105 people. I was quite flabbergasted and said immediately that it was impossible! But they told me that the ticket was already paid for and all arrangements made. When I really believed it, I was overjoyed and full of plans. I went back to Rochester to get the clothes I wanted at the store on East Avenue where I used to shop. I still remember the suit woven with threads of very light gray and pale rose that was so beautiful that I parted with it years later quite reluctantly.

And now it was three days before I was to proceed to Canada to Quebec to sail out the St. Lawrence in the SS Metagama with the Dr. Flick party bound for a landing in Italy. I was excitedly happy. Coming home from downtown, I got on the Westcott streetcar. The motorman I didn't know, but the conductor who took the tokens was the one who'd been on the line for a number of years. He knew all the regular customers and amused them by holding them at the coin box with his newest story. I laughed heartily and went to a seat.

I had not noticed any other passengers. A tall young man arose and came over and said, "Would you mind if I talked to you?" I had no idea who he was, whether I wanted to or even should talk to him, but he sat down and we visited. He found out I was going to Europe with the Flick's, whom he knew well. He asked what my husband did and I told him he wasn't living. Finally, he asked my name and when I answered "Grace Tobey Lockwood," a queer surprised questioning expression came on his face that I did not understand. He asked if I'd send him a card from the Eiffel Tower in Paris. I agreed, but said I didn't know his name. I wrote into my address book "James Russell Paine" and very quickly forgot all about him until opening the same little book sometime later found his name and I inwardly thought, "Oh! That man on the streetcar!" And knowing that the Eiffel Tower was closed for repair, kept my word and sent the card from Italy.

The trip thru Italy, Switzerland, Germany, Holland, Belgium, France, England, Wales and Scotland was thrillingly interesting. Somewhere it is, at least partially, written up. I do not feel at the moment it should be written here. I might add a few personal notes, however. I loved the sea and I did not become seasick. Looking over the rails, I watched the water for hours. We played shuffleboard, took deck walks and spent eighteen days aboard because delay was caused by the breakdown of an engine. It was so enjoyable that we were almost reluctant to reach land in Naples, Italy. Naples, Rome, Pompeii and Herculanen-Firenza (Florence), Venice, Lake Como, etc. all so foreign to previous experience that I found it difficult to make my mother and father see it all with my eyes when I returned home. We seemed to visit all the cathedrals and art galleries in Europe as well as the ruins, archeological findings and places of beauty and historical significance. It was a tremendously large group for the Flick's to manage but all went very smoothly. All reservations were cleared in advance and a number of young college men earned their way by caring for details, baggage, tickets, etc.

I had had no real experience in the art world until then, so a new world was opened to me. I had tried a little sketching and a bit of watercolor, all inexperienced and immature but now I was seeing masters of that tremendous field. Probably the Louvre, the Uffizi and the galleries in Italy, Holland, and France stand out in memory most clearly. To the area of Naples was added trips to Amalfi, Sorrento, Pompeii and some went to Vesuvius. In Rome the famed ruins included the Coliseum on The Appian Way, we saw the trees of which are still sharply recalled. I loved Florence (Firenza) and St. Marks Square, the pigeons, the gondolas in Venice; the Fieta in St. Marks Cathedral, exquisite in marble and beauty. All breathtaking experiences. I recall vividly the red-sashed gondoliers on the Grand Canal, the Bridge of Sighs, the Rialto Bridge, the Venetian glass makers.

On to Lake Maggiore and Lake Como and then into Switzerland to see Lucerne, climb the Rigikulm in cable cars, pick edelweiss and look out over the world of snow clad peaks and entrancing vistas. On to Lucarno in Switzerland with its characteristic flavor so different from Italy. It never failed to astonish me how the atmosphere of one country could change so markedly in such short distances.

At Munich, Germany, we saw the day long giving of the famous Passionspiele, an outstanding experience with Anton Lang taking the part of Christ. It was here that I purchased the first doll for Janie.

While in Munich, my birthday came on August 3rd. I had a birthday party to which I invited ten of those who had become closest to me. We ordered what we wanted to eat and for fun, we had steins of beer at the famous Hof Brau Haus. At another table a young German with a red nose, unasked, cut my silhouette and presented it to me with a low bow and what was probably a beautiful speech but to my ears not understandable. I was quite surprised! But the greatest surprise of all came when I got the bill! You'll have to recall that after World War I, an American dollar was worth a bushel of German marks (I'm exaggerating, of course). That evening, dinner for ten people cost me a little over $1.50 total.

We went to Holland, and saw in Amsterdam the famous tulip beds and the historic dikes to hold back the sea.

In Syracuse, I had met an Edmund Van Malderghem whom my mother was interested in because of his music. He wished me to go to Belgium to visit his relatives there. In our Flick party there were twins, one of them consented to go with me. We took a train to Ghent and arrived safely. The family was very interested in us and served us a wonderful dinner but though we tried halting German and French, neither group could understand the other. But their warm-hearted reception was very evident.

In Paris, we stayed several days in a hotel near The Montmarte. One of the days we spent in The Louvre, an extremely art educational day of beauty. Another occasion, we visited the Grand Opera and invaded the Folies Bergere. We danced in Paris, drank French wines and champagne. At moments, the younger ones of the party flirted outrageously with the young Frenchmen but were wary of them as well. They enjoyed it – so did we.

The Flick's took the party to the American Cemeteries with their rows and rows of white crosses. At Verdun, Chateau Thierry, Dijon and Nevers we sobbed unrestrainedly. It seemed such a waste of the lives of the best of American young men.

On the London, London Bridge, Big Ben, the Tower of London, the Crown Jewels, etc. In front of Buckingham Palace we unsuccessfully tried to make the Palace Guards smile, but they stood at attention with unblinking eyes like gaily dressed wooden soldiers.

Moving toward our coming departure, we visited Llandudno Beach in Wales, saw the heather of Scotland and rode a tallyho with tiered seats. Our final visit in Europe was to the Castle at Edinburgh. Then to our waiting ship. This is an extremely sketchy account which is better written elsewhere.

Family and friends wanted me to bring back the amount allowed of $100 in loot. I found I had to pay customs which I didn't expect. The party all except me stayed on the boat to Montreal. I got off at Quebec and took the train to Syracuse, arriving ahead of the Flick party. I was so anxious to see Janet and give her the doll which I had carried in my arms since Holland (it couldn't be added to the over-filled suitcase).

A newspaper reporter found I was at home and came to interview me about the trip. A long article appeared in the morning paper. I'd had a wonderful time but was glad to get home. It seemed ages longer than three months.

That evening there was a phone call. I said, "Who is this?" "JRP," was the answer. "I don't know any JRP," I said. "Yes, you do!" Finally I tumbled, "Oh! The Eiffel Tower Man." I had forgotten him entirely. The trip was too full of sights and new experiences. He came over to the house in a brand new plaid overcoat. We took a long walk and I told him of the trip. Near the end, he asked me if I would consider being his girl so he could see me frequently. I said I'd be his sister if he wished and he replied emphatically that he didn't want a sister! He told me later that he'd fallen in love with me on the streetcar and came near to joining the Flick party to keep near me and was on pins and needles all the summer for fear I'd fall in love with someone else. On the walk he wanted to ask me to marry him but thought it too soon.

It was late September. I took the Americanization League County Organizer job on October 1st, and Florence stayed on a month to see that everything was to go smoothly. J. Russell followed me everywhere. He popped up every noon to take me to the Salina Street Chinese restaurant to eat. On October 1ˢᵗ, while eating there, he said, "I wish we'd been married ten years and were sitting here as we are now." "Why! Russell, you don't even know me!" I said. "Oh! Yes I do!" he fired back. I couldn't answer that one. I had a very strong idea that I would never marry again.

After I returned from Europe, I had several young men friends whom J. Russell tried continually to get ahead of. He wanted to tie all my time up with him. I had a job to do and I was determined to do it well. It involved visiting schools in the evenings, conferences, meetings, naturalization courts, and more. J. R. managed to go along most of the time. He was helpful, companionable. He loved Janet and she him. He carried her around on his shoulders and played with her. She got to calling him her Daddy. I didn't disillusion her. She'd never known her own. The demands of the job were excessive. J. Russell asked me to please marry him. I was deeply troubled, I didn't want to be unfair to him. We talked it over many times. I told him I was all mixed up. Could I really love two people? The first marriage had been so complete, so happy. "I would not marry anyone," I said actually trembling, "Unless I was certain of myself." The days went by.

PART IV

In September, as home-going neared, the breezes would send the drying leaves scurrying up the sandy shores, the gulls cry would become a longer wail and grayer, heavier clouds would pass majestically overhead. As if with a triumphal chord, all nature would burst into a colorful out-giving and fading go to sleep for its period of rest.

Chapter 7

Charles Butler and J. Russell had been in college at Syracuse University together, had roomed in Sims Hall and graduated in the same year, 1911. The Butler's had lived at 113 Trinity Place nearly opposite to Russell's mother and stepfather, Mr. Ezra Bryan. The Butler's had moved to Baltimore, Maryland, where Charles had opened a laundry. He wrote to Russell to come down and help him get it started. Troubled and distracted by Russell's constant attention, I urged him to go. He went reluctantly. Later he said he thought he had lost out with me completely. He wrote frequently and I answered.

One day in March, I was at Borodino to see a foreign born non-citizen family about papers. Dr. Paul Paine, Syracuse Librarian, asked me to stop to see Mr. Jerome to ask if a branch library was needed in his town. The Jerome's begged me to stay overnight as a real blizzard had come up, but I was determined to go home. In the long ride downhill to Otisco Lake, I could not see the road, the car slowed down and down, fighting the drifts. One place it almost

147

stopped. I could see nothing, but gradually I made it. A letter from Russell said he was sitting on the capital steps in Washington in his shirtsleeves on that very day.

With J. Russell away, I could get a better perspective on things. I realized I missed him and discovered Janet did too. After a long night of thinking, I drew a line figure of a little girl with tears running down her face – nothing else. Charles Butler handed him that letter, and within fifteen minutes, Russell was bound for New York and then Syracuse. He telegraphed me to meet him at the station. I can still remember the strength of that bear hug when he stepped from the train. I no longer doubted. It *was* possible to love two people, enough to marry them both, but it would not be quite the same.

As the wedding day approached, Janet became ill. She slept all the time for four days. The family was quite frantic. Sleeping sickness and other things were considered. I told the doctor that we must postpone the wedding until she was better. He said, "Never postpone a wedding. Go ahead, I think she'll be O. K." I had made a very pale pink organdy dress for her with ruffles at the neck and sleeves and a very full skirt. She had seen it and loved it. It was planned that she as to be the ring bearer, carrying it on a small pillow. On the day of the wedding, she roused and was carried into the living room and placed in a small rocking chair (which is now at Janet's). Reverend L. P. Tucker was to be our minister. J. Russell told him to take the "obey" out of the service, as no woman was going to have to obey him. Reverend Tucker was very conventional in his thinking. He left it out but didn't like the changing of the wording.

The Americanization League was invited. Joyce Holmes was there to get our wedding breakfast. Sed

Senigo Sanford, Russell's cousin came from Wilkes Barre to sing. I had quite recently met J. R.'s mother and stepfather. It was explained to me by the Butler's that J. R.'s mother had tried to play matchmaker so many times that when he really meant business, he wanted to be on his own, so I was not introduced until nearly time for the wedding. It was a beautiful day and all went well. Our car was placed in Dr. Curtis' garage on Westcott Street back of our yard. The folks had not found it. We rushed out thru the back, got it and drove out so quickly we didn't hear the gasp of alarm behind us. In our haste, one wheel had just escaped, going over the wall that separated the yards.

On top of Westminster Hill, we shook off the confetti and rice and started for Rochester. We had not planned to go far but intended to call home to see if Janet continued to be all right. We got to talking and found ourselves on the wrong road, arriving at Clifton Springs Sanatorium. J. R. said that was a hotel as well as a health resort so we parked the car, planning to stay overnight and call home.

As we came up the steps, a Mrs. Spaulding came forward to greet Russell. Her husband was a patient and a Rotarian friend. I stood back of Russell and the conversation continued on and on without my being introduced. I wondered, but kept still but was reading the expression on Mrs. Spaulding's face. What was she thinking about Russell was unmistakable! Finally, it had gone on long enough and Russell turned to me and said, "I want you to meet my wife." "Your wife! Why Russell, you aren't married!" Russell said, "Yes." They asked, ""When?" "This morning, several hours ago." Russ said he'd done it all on purpose because he'd caught what they were thinking. Mrs. Spaulding as if to make amends insisted that we go to the movies that evening. When we came down in the morning, I realized she had told the whole dining room. All attention was directed our way. Again, I wish I hadn't the habit of blushing so easily.

We went on to Rochester to the Powers Hotel. At breakfast about noon the next day we ran into a restaurant waiter who knew J. R. Again I was put thru a similar experience as with the Spaulding's, only this time I understood.

We both returned to our work on Monday, Russell to J. K. Rush Camping Equipment and I to the County work. We lived for a time at my parents' house and later moved two doors north at Mrs. Green's home in the lower apartment. Janet divided her time between the houses, at home in either. When she started kindergarten at Edward Smith School, the teacher asked her for her name. She said, "My name's Paine now, cause me and mother married Daddy." The teacher said she was glad she knew the circumstances.

On May 3rd, 1923, when we were married, I was 26 and J. Russell was 32. We were married before Florence and Silas were.

Now is the time to explain the expression on Russell's face on the streetcar when I first told him my name. The facts put together were these. He had seen Janet as a three year old and me walking on Euclid Avenue. I had not noticed him. He was attracted to us but didn't know who we were. He told me that he thought to himself, "I'd like to marry a girl like that one." On Trinity Place in another place there was a couple named Morton and Ethel Schiele. They used to invite J. Russell to go along on outings with them and Morton's sister. Russell was called the "Batch." One day, Ethel asked Russell playfully when he was going to get married. He answered in the same spirit, "When I meet a rich young widow." Ethel said I know a young widow (not rich) who married a friend of mine whose home was next to ours on Baker Avenue. He died in the war. She is Grace Tobey Lockwood. Russell remembered the name.

Very shortly after, he attended the Little Theater on East Fayette Street and saw the play *Why The Chimes Rang*. In it, I was an old lady with white hair leaning on a cane. The name on the program was Grace Tobey Lockwood. Two weeks alter, I was given a similar part in a second play and again he saw my name. I must have been convincing, for now he was certain that the Schiele's were "ribbing" him. But when I said on the streetcar in 1922 that I was Grace Tobey Lockwood, he was quite surprised and startled. Destiny working out again.

Jan was great company for her Todey and Aunt Minnie especially when my father was on the road and I was working. By now it was a very natural arrangement. Janet replaced my sister Helen. Aunt Minnie had come to live with us after Grandma Holmes died. Marnie finished college. Joyce came and transferred to Cornell University. June Reed Babcock came occasionally to see us but finally moved to Portland, Oregon. She felt she would secure more pupils there. Before she went, June and Bill gave a concert in Walton, New York. My father and Kaveda

Holmes made the arrangements. Joe Donovan went to California. After June was gone, Lee Gonter joined up with Bill in the Sutfin Block. I think June regretted going very much but there was no money to bring her back and she was gradually losing her ability to play violin due to arthritis in her fingers. She wrote my parents continuously. My father often had to finance her. She didn't come back to Wellsville, for by now Lee and Bill were sharing very small quarters.

June's beautiful Stradivarius was finally sold. I think it broke her heart to part with it for she died in Portland not long after. At the time in Wellsville only Bill and Lee, Bessie and Bessie's June, John Cline and Velma remained. All the rest were gone or scattered. Today in 1967, only Bessie Babcock and her June are left. In Downsville, the only relative who remains is Maude Holmes. In Walton, there is only Douglas Nutt and Anna Tobey Martin's son. Change is the pattern of life.

Chapter 8

At Mrs. Green's house we rented the bedroom located off the living room to two University students, "Rusty" Scribner and Morris Meyers, two very fine likeable young men.

Jan played very happily between the two houses, 733 and 741 Maryland Avenue, having her own room in each. J. Russell had left me free to work or not to, as I pleased. Because the County Organizer job of the Americanization League was so full of interest, problems and personalities, I was reluctant to stop work, so I continued. J. Russell reactivated the Syracuse Soap Company on Fayette Street after his return from World War I. He found that the organization of The Clark Music Store had changed markedly. Before the war, he had been the head of the Clark Harp Company, selling harps, large ones and Melville Clark's small Irish harps during which time he had on occasion traveled across the United States and to Europe in 1913, taking harps and a blind man, John Fowler, with him. His story of those trips would make a very interesting addition to this writing. I should also like to add his war experience, his organization of the first ambulance corp. to leave Syracuse with which he expected to go but his draft came sooner and a trip to Washington, D. C. proved futile to change the picture, of his time at Gettysburg where Eisenhower was in command, of his letters and orders signed by Eisenhower, of his eventual work with troops generally thought of as misfits needing special training; his newspaper work while in service, his promotion to First Lieutenant, etc.

Because there was no work at Clark's Music Store and the Harp Department had been absorbed into the general music department, J. Russell turned to soap making and selling, at first in the area where the Chimes Building now stands at the corner of West Onondaga and South Salina Street. He also had a period of working with Rush Camping Equipment but finally reactivated the Soap Company, no longer making soap but became a jobber of soap, soap products, sanitary supplies, and the like. As it was the days of house to house salesmen, he also had many articles which these people could buy wholesale and resell.

J. Russell has the notable characteristic of being the friend and having a deep interested in the underdog, the misfit, even those out of jail, the drifters. He gave them no sympathy but would be more apt to say, "Come on now, you've the ability to accomplish better things – now go do it." From him, they could take it, his optimistic joking, his friendly uplifting philosophy. I do not mean to convey that all customers were of this type but these were the ones whom J. Russell felt a purpose in assisting.

From the Fayette Street store which was heated in winter only by a pot-bellied stove, the room hot near it and very cold away from it. The store was moved finally to 252

Washington Street, a former part of the Howard Hotel, and remained there until its dissolution in 1958. As a jobber, J. R. increased the number of items handled and enlarged the stock mostly for wholesale distribution.

In 1924, I kept working as long as was possible before the birth of our first son but had to turn over the County job to another though; finally though, I was asked to continue as assistant to the new head. Names entering now and thru the years are Helen Valentine, Esther Heefner, Fredericka Zeeb, Marion O'Neil, Angie Di Florio, and Janet H. Lockwood (Paine) Wells.

One night I awakened J. R. and said, "This is it! Get me to the hospital." He helped me dress and went to get the car, garaged midway up Redfield Place. He was gone and gone and I became quite anxious with the passing of the minutes. Finally he showed up. The car had had a flat tire – of all times! I was driven to the Syracuse Memorial Hospital, then on West Genesee Street, and on October 24th, our son, a nine pound boy was born, J. Russell Paine Jr. III.

Scribner & Meyers had been around the night we left and were extremely interested in the little son now added to the apartment. Janet was excited and very proud of her brother. She was now seven years old. As I was at home most of the time, she skipped between the houses but spent more of her time with us. Her Todey was not always too pleased about this.

One evening, Mrs. Greene knocked on the door and to our surprise asked that Janet be told she must stay more with her grandmother. Her running in and out of the back door was annoying to her. I flared at that and said, "Janie is my daughter. She will be with me all she likes!"

Furthermore, I give you notice right now. We will move by the first of next month." I think J. Russell was surprised at the force of those words but he backed me up 100%.

We went out the next day and looked for a place to buy, as that had become our decision. On the first of the month, we were in 710 Westcott Street, just around the corner on the street parallel to Maryland. The Charles Conner family lived upstairs. Marjorie was their only child when we came. Jan, Russ, and Marjorie played together. Jan contrived many doings to interest them.

Being of a restless disposition and because circumstances prevented me from having a full-time position at the Americanization League County Department, I taught evening school Americanization classes in various villages in the county and Saturday Citizenship class at the League office. J. Russell would be at home or one of the three older women: Todey, Aunt Minnie or Russell's mother Mrs. Bryan would help when needed. Every time I thought of stepping out completely I was encouraged to continue.

But another break came. On October 19, 1927, our Frank Tobey Paine was born again at the same hospital – again in the same room. Before this event, another of those crystal clear unsought experiences came. It was cold, and I sat on a cushion near the furnace register (coal fire) to get my feet warm. This pregnancy had been a difficult one. I had 2 months of extreme nausea finally overcome by a M. D. not my own, but the doctor-uncle of Florence Conner

156

who had become a close friend. I suppose it may have been unethical for him to step in but he was greatly disturbed to see the condition continue for so long.

Later, as I sat on the cushion alone it seemed as if a voice spoke to my brain (not my ears), asking if I wished to continue life. I could now leave it, if I wished to. Horrified, I jumped to my feet and strenuously affirmed my desire to continue it; too many people needed me, I thought. What if there were difficulties! Somehow I'd manage. I settled down in confidence.

In the hospital that October day, I was told I had a nine pound, ten ounce boy, named for my father Frank Tobey. J. Russell told me that Dr. Schoeneck and Dr. Hughes had said we must not have any more children; that the birth had been so difficult that for quite a time it had been a choice as which one to save, mother or child or perhaps they couldn't save either. Dr. Jones had told me when Russ was born that I had interlocking pelvic bones. Before Frank was born Dr. Jones died. I had told Dr. Schoeneck what Jones had said but intuitively felt I wasn't believe entirely but was perhaps using imagination. Caesarean section should have been the method with Frank but it was a relatively new process and not in general usage.

Years later Dr. Hughes told Frank of his experiences at this birth, approximately his first birth as assistant to Dr. Schoeneck. Dr. Hughes felt he never would forget it. Dr. Hughes, Frank, and Johanne (Frank's wife) were all members of St. Paul's Episcopalian Church when he told Frank of the experiences at his birth.

Eleanor Conner was born to the Conner's upstairs. Now there were four little ones and Janet in the house. All had splendid times playing together as they grew. In spite of this continued activity and duties at home, I continued teaching night classes. J. Russell, Sr. was a wonderful help. He always has loved children. He took over the night duties giving me the day. He could return to sleep within moments. If awakened, I would take hours to get to sleep again. I tremendously appreciated his help.

Scribners & Meyers rented a flat on Maryland Avenue hill and move away from our house. I decided to open a gift shop in the front parlor. Why I thought I could undertake anything more I don't know but it flourished. All friends, relatives, and acquaintances brought their art and craft work there to be sold on commission collected by me. I called it Janet's Gift Shop. She helped with the selling, as she felt a partnership in the undertaking. It was continued about three years.

On Sundays regularly (too regularly it seemed), we were expected to dinner at Mr. and Mrs. Ezra Bryan's at 113 Trinity Place. J. Russell's mother gave elaborate dinners. J. R.'s stepfather was a very jolly person and enjoyed the company. His presence dominated the table. He seemed always happy and had excellent health. Thru him, the two were Christian Scientists. Julia Howland, an adopted daughter, was married and her family was also Scientists. I couldn't help but think that their positive attitude toward health was well demonstrated in results.

I pleased Mr. Bryan one day by giving him a Harry Lauder record. He loved it and played it on his phonograph repeatedly. At home, we had our first radio, a small hand size crystal set. How excited we all were when KDKA came in clearly. It was considered a modern miracle!

There were happy years, all be it they were busy. Frank rode his red and white kiddie car. Russ started school at Sumner off of Beech Street. He loved it. Jan had Margaret Murray, Margart Butler, Emily Hugadom and others to play with out of doors or in the attic. The Conner children were at our flat and ours at theirs constantly. It seemed all one happy family. If I had errands downtown, Florence took care of the bunch. If Florence was away, I took over.

One Sunday, we went to the Bryan's as usual. All was happy and merry, also as usual. As Mr. Bryan was talking, a sudden flash of intuition told me it would be the last time we would all be there together. Startled, I kept my head down so no one would see the change in expression. The perception told me the area of difficulty was around Mr. Bryan. At that dinner my mother, father, and aunt were also present. I didn't want my mother in particular to see my expression for she was the most knowledgeable as to what it might mean.

When home, I said, "Mother, take this envelope but don't open it until next Sunday." "Why?" she said. "Just wait and see," I said. It was the first time I'd decided to write down these previsions.

On the Thursday of that very week, Mr. Bryan went into the upstairs bathroom and dropped to the floor dead. There were no more dinners at Trinity Place. Most of the house as rented to a family. Space was no longer available.

Mother opened the note. It said, "This is the last of the Sunday dinners at this house. The difficulty indicated is Mr. Bryan."

When I was real young, my sensitivities in this direction were spoken of as the result of over imagination. At times, I'd even been spanked for it. I grew to let it happen but to enclose it within myself and let myself note how correct it could be. It was an inward game. But, I confess, I was glad when I saw that it happened to other people. I would hear people say things such as the following: *I knew who was on the phone before I lifted the receiver. I felt the letter had bad news in it. I knew you'd stop in today. I have a feeling he won't live too long. I felt it meant trouble. I knew I was safe, I would not get killed in the war. I feel as if trouble of some kind is coming. Something inward told me not to take that train.* Later I learned that it was the developing sixth sense in man, the intuitive one.

The out of the ordinary, the incredible, men of science have thought beneath their dignity to verify, so convinced are they of their impossibility. There is no effect without a cause. Man is the least known of all beings. Man is dual or triplex - yet his whole nature is a mystery to him. He thinks, but just what is thought? No one can say. Will is an immaterial force, all soul faculties are immaterial. Nevertheless, if I *will* to move my arm, my will moves matter. How does it act? What is the mediators between mind and muscle? As yet no one can say. How does the optic nerve transmit to the brain the perception of external objects?

The force of electricity or of steam was once ridiculed, yet today they motivate extensively the outward workings of man. Though differing essentially from these forces, the still little psychic force exists seemingly spontaneous and still uncontrollable by man except in outstanding exceptional individuals, but still spasmodic and unexpected by the majority. However, it is a developing force called by some the sixth sense, now slowly coming into being as the other senses came, by long evolutionary process. This is evidenced by the "hunch," the "I have a feeling" and other phenomena and slowly, so slowly, being accepted under the classification as E. S. P.

To Camille Flammarion, French scientist, goes the distinction of the name of psychic forces and classified by him as relating to the Psyche, or soul of man. There are elements in man to study, to analyze, elements unexplained and which we at present assign to the psychic realm.

As to the psychological question of the Soul and the analysis of spiritual forces, we are still babes in thought and scientific proof. We just don't know, but the beginnings of knowledge are faintly discernible. It is irrational to deny what we do not understand. It is irrational to over-develop gullibility without solid basis of investigation. The mind must sense the truth. Preconceived ideas close gates to further knowledge. To deny and prejudge has never proved anything.

I write this, probably, because it has seemed necessary at times to defend telepathy, clairvoyance, prevision and all classifications now designated as E. S. P.

Sumner School phoned. Would I come and get Russ. It was thought that he had measles. It was a bitter cold day. I walked the poor child home. Measles were evident. I had no use of a car at that time and our finances had made a taxi a very unusual occurrence. He was a very sick child for weeks after that and finally went into shooting temperatures up high and then down again. Our medical doctor didn't seem to help. When he complained of his ears, I got a specialist, Dr. Roy Seely Moore, to come. He took him immediately to the hospital. He was put in a ward with other children. He looked so pitiful. The long bout with temperatures and loss of weight brought him down to 48 pounds. He begged us to stay. The hospital wouldn't allow it. I felt miserable. Russell took me to a movie thinking it would help us. I couldn't see anything but that little face with the beseeching eyes. Dr. Moore said measles had given him mastoid on both sides and now the infection had gone into blood poisoning. I insisted on a private room so I could stay near or with Russ. I read stories, made up stories and tried for his comfort. It was still not the time for the wonder drugs.

Dr. Moore was a medical doctor with his heart deep in his work. He told us later that he stayed up all one night restudying all the medical books available to try to save Russ' life. One day J. Russell came to the hospital from the store. He was detained in the hallway by Dr. Moore and two other doctors. I was called out to join them. Dr. Moore tried to break the news to me that Russ could not live. It was the opinion of all three. "But he will," I said, "You wait and see!" To convince me, I was taken to the hospital laboratory and showed a test tube of blood from Russ, two-thirds of it pus. I looked at it. "Yes, I see," I said, "But he will live." They gave up trying to convince me.

That night I told Russ we had a war on our hands. The white army in his blood was trying to beat the red army. The red army just had to win. Would he help me? We talked, we read stories. He finally went to sleep. I held his hand for the rest of the night. Toward morning I felt the heat in that little hand was less. When the nurse took his temperature, it had dropped from 104, 105, 106, even 107 for moments, to 101. She looked astonished! Dr. Moore and the other doctors came. Dr. Moore said, "We sometimes see miracles happen in the hospital. This is certainly one." I said, "I *knew* he'd get well." They looked at me thoughtfully.

Russ finally came home a mere skeleton, weak and uncertain. He had to be taught to walk again. It didn't seem possible, but it was. Gradually, he was back to normal. Thru the summer we kept him in the sun as much as possible.

On Halloween night, the Conner children and Russ and Frank were in bed after an evening of dress-up. Jan might have been up. Mr. and Mrs. Conner and J. Russell and I were seated in the dining room chatting and playing some kind of card game. All of a sudden, startling us, Mr. Conner jumped up and raced up the stairs. What was that for, we asked ourselves. He came downstairs, very white and upset. He said while he was playing he had a vivid picture presented to him of Eleanor in bed with the curtains on fire over her little head. He seemed to feel as if catapulted out of the room. Eleanor lay there sleeping peacefully but the lace curtains *were* afire over her head. The wind had blown the curtains over a still lit jack o' lantern.

The Conner's were very close friends and J. Russell was in an awkward position. Charles business was poor, very poor, at times. He was an engraver. They were months and months behind on the rent which was making it more and more difficult for us to meet the mortgage payments, interest and other expenses on the house. The Conner's gave us notes in lieu of payment but that didn't help in the immediate present.

Something has just happened this March day, 1967, which I somehow feel to be intended directly for me. During the time I wrote about my father and mother's interest in Spiritualism, I deeply wished for several days that I could talk to them about their interest in the subject. I felt deeply sorry that I had been so young when their thoughts had turned so definitely in this direction. Later years had brought me knowledge of scientific investigations, attempts to discredit, acceptance by many prominent people and the knowledge of many fraudulent mediums. Like all new things, negative approach precedes acceptance if scientific proof becomes available.

Within a day or two, Janet walked into the house with a slender book in her hand, titled *The Salem Seer* by Bartlett. "I don't want it," she said, handing it to me. It is not a new book, no date, pages discolored. The first sentence reads, "I met Charles H. Foster, the famous Spiritual Medium in 1870 --- in New York City." My father's name is not in it but some notes in his writing are. Thus I know it to be his. I have never seen it before, nor read it anywhere. Some of my parents things went to the Wells' house when Jan and Howie left Maryland Avenue for their new Fayetteville one. As a matter of fact, Charles H. Foster is a name entirely new to me.

As this is so characteristic, happening at other times, I note it here. When deeply desiring a book, or knowledge of a fact, it is placed before me. Coincidence, you might say – but its very repetition denies it. A dear friend of mine, Mabel Burlingham, repeatedly had the same happen to her. Perhaps to those who feel that space is not unoccupied, who are certain of immortality, who vibrate to unseen-by-the-eye influences create a channel. This is something again that I'd like explained though the truth of it is unquestioned by me.

I do not ask for psychic experiences, cannot control them by willing their happening. To answer for myself, I'd say, it is intuitional perception, a characteristic which is developing in man, generally. Coming thru the ages with first one, then two, then gradually developing to the point of five senses, we now move slowly into the sixth. Furthermore, all living now have some of this in them, deny it or not. It is evident in the hunch, the feeling that something is so, without reason to substantiate it. In the knowing who is calling on the phone, in thinking of a person and receiving a letter from him. And even in foreknowledge of events. The most reluctant to admit it only have to know themselves better. The faculty is a natural part of the mind abilities. The developing awareness in the brain lies behind it. The psychiatrists are often the most doubtful on the subject, some thinking it a psychotic abnormality – but the world once thought the earth to be flat.

The book brought to me is one on which I can see and feel my father's interest, his doubt as well as his final saying as we now do with Flying Saucers, "There definitely seems to be (as yet the unexplained) something to the subject."

I've searched thru the years for answers in this direction. It is substantiated by the library of books in my home. No larger in number, or wider in interests and scope, exists elsewhere in Syracuse. I hope to be led to the proper housing of them after I step out. My search for that person or organization which will realize their value and keep them intact (except for judicial and definite return loaning as a

165

reference library). Even my immediate family do not seem to realize the depth of this desire.

At the moment, I feel that I could write a second book based upon this subject and perhaps make it quite interesting if I could base it upon personal experiences. In 1967, one can speak in this direction with more assurance of acceptance and understanding. We have moved a great way in knowledge since the days of the Salem witches and intolerance though even ten years ago one spoke of psychism quietly to those of like experience and avoided the conversations, questionings and the subjecting to not-quite-right-in-the-head conclusions of those who had no real experience or who sloughed it off as imagination, hallucinations, fancy or mind distortion. I cannot feel that psychiatry will fully understand until the whole subject of continuity of life is understood, the electrical vibratory rate of individuals; the separation of earth into three-dimensional existence and because of it, man's inability to understand the fourth-dimensional world we are born into when we experience the "death" out of this; of the reincarnation of the Ego of man into another "day" in the school of life by return to earth; of the goals of man's development and the definite understanding of God's plan of existence. How far we are from that I cannot guess but it seems each so-called "new discovery" goes thru stages of general skepticism, ridicule, and finally general acceptance – the negative to the positive.

Chapter 9

Grandma Bryan came with news that Dr. Todd's cottage at Sandy Pond was for sale. Dr. Todd was a neighbor on Trinity Place. Wouldn't we go see it? It was proposed that if we liked it, we would split the cost six ways and all use it. Mr. and Mrs. Tobey, Miss Minnie Holmes, J. Russell and I. It seemed a far-fetched idea. However, that Sunday was a gloriously beautiful day. We drove to Parson's farm at Sandy Pond. Dr. Todd had a roomy in-board motorboat awaiting us. We crossed the one and a half miles to the camp and landed on the "bay." It was a slight climb up the hill to the cottage past the outdoor pump. As I raced to the top and looked beyond the cottage to the wide expanse of Lake Ontario stretching way out to infinity, I shouted out loud for joy, "Oh, let's let it be ours!" So it was purchased. It must have been in September of 1928, for Frank was only eleven months old when we first went, tying him by a clothes line to the porch so he would not fall down the fairly high bank to the water.

The camp at Sandy Pond having been jointly purchased by Mr. and Mrs. Frank W. Tobey, Miss Minnie A. Holmes, Mrs. Ezra Bryan, and Mr. and Mrs. J. Russell Paine, it continued to furnish summer vacations for this group, children and friends until about 1950. Situated on the largely sand and trees peninsula paralleling the north-south shore of Lake Ontario, its lot embraced 250 feet on the lake and on Sandy Pond, with 1800 feet between. Prosaic facts do not reveal the beauty. When the sun shone its glimmerings twinkled over the gentle in-rolling waves. The noisy gulls and the sound of the unceasing lapping of the waters engraved an unforgettable memory.

The cottage was crude. Daylight could be seen thru the sidings. There were bunk beds as well as built-in or movable single beds. Two "bedrooms" had three-quarter sides. A loft over the porch had a floor mattress. Incredibly, we slept twelve on some occasions. A three burner Coleman stove furnished the meals. Water came up from the pump halfway down the hill. We had a "dining table" with benches, a "living room table" with kerosene lamps for reading or game playing and one early vintage radio to keep us in touch with the world.

We were on a sand bluff overlooking the lake and in a group of some forty trees, only one was large near the porch steps and one a sturdy hard cherry which resisted all the severe winter storm efforts to tip it over onto the cottage. We were a quarter mile from the channel that cut thru from the lake to the pond. Early morning brought the fishermen in their boats thru into the lake. Ackerman's, the Comfort Hotel, Seiber Shores, and The Elms were cottager's havens on the mainland. But out where we were two miles across the pond, our nearest neighbor (at first) was over a mile away at Hawkin's down the sand peninsula. A two mile shore walk north brought us to a rocky road which led east to the Parson's farm. We often walked down there for mail, use of phone or, on occasion, to get help. In the early days, we drove the car there and left it in the woods beyond the fence, then walked out. Those who could not walk were rowed over in the boat with supplies and provisions. Until 1931, Dad struggled with the in-board motorboat and we did have some splendid rides in it around the pond. But it was cantankerous and gave him lots of trouble. A New England dory came into our possession, which was a curiosity to all who saw it as it was narrowed at each end.

It wasn't long, with my penchant for severe sunburn, before I had cleared a path thru alder trees where I could find a shady place and still drink in the warmth from the sun and earth. The dock for the boat and the path up to the cottage ran out of this area.

Each of us had two or three swimsuits. We were in and out of the water many times a day. One suit was always drying. We scarcely had on shoes all summer. Exploring the peninsula, picking berries, running the boat going to Ackerman's, swimming the channel, entertaining friends, playing ball, and playing croquet, we passed the time. On rainy days, we played games inside and read stories. Once or twice a summer, the three days storm came. Then ones' ingenuity was taxed to keep things interesting and to keep warm, as there was no heat. The waves were too high on lake or pond to leave and no one ventured over.

Nights were for campfires, marshmallow roasts, telling stories and for sing fests.

As the children grew, the Conner's were there often as playmates and Janet brought her special girl friends. I was very happy to be with them. Schools were closed and also evening school programs. For at least eight weeks, I was free. J. Russell and Dad joined us on weekends. J. Russell was *very* reluctant to leave on Monday mornings to return to work; at times to the point of being quite cross about it, but the store needed him. The children and his mother needed me so we had to look forward to the long weekends. Often Aunt Minnie was with us. She and Grandma Bryan took long walks to the channel and back, especially at sunset. I can mentally see them stopping to talk thru "Grandma" Bryan's ear trumpet and later ear phone, an elongated tube from ear to mouthpiece, held close to the other person. These contraptions amused the children. I never saw, before or after, anything like them.

My mother came infrequently. She didn't understand why one had to leave a comfortable home with all conveniences to be happy in such a remote water-surrounded place full of problems and make-shifts. The children especially loved it: they fished, lived close to nature, discovered the life cycle of the frogs, watched a family of skunks walk thru the yard, climbed trees, rolled down sand hills, built things with wood and sand, and passed the days in happy contentment.

There were times when the responsibility sat heavy on my shoulders, times of being a bit lonely for folks my own age but also moments when the consciousness sailed out in wondrous expansion in response to the sky. Then I would dream of the higher purposes, of interminable ages past and future and feel lifted spiritually into the beauty of gorgeous sunsets. At such times I would sketch, write or devise poems and express those wellings-up of soul to beauty.

With the children, we played a game each night of fair weather. Get ready for bed, brush teeth, finish the water drinking, then go and sit in a row in pajamas or nighties on

170

top of the sand hill and watch the sun go down. They grew to love this and the colors and would attempt painting it on rainy days in water colors when we were not playing Parcheesi, Old Maid, Checkers, or Flinch.

All was so peaceful that I required personal harmony as well, no noisy arguments, no fights except in fun, no wrangles. The offender was promptly set aside until he or she felt that it was not the way. It was too bad that I could not have carried this rule thru for myself in later years when, driven into physical exhaustion by the accumulating and pressing events, I sometimes exploded into irritability. It was like letting off compressed steam. It always astonished people who didn't expect it. By that time, I had found there was a physical breaking point in us all.

Tarzan was very much in the minds of the young folks at the time of which I write. Russ asked me one day to buy some fur with spots like a leopard and make Tarzan suits for him and Frank. His heart was so set on this idea that I had difficulty in changing fur to cloth, which I explained would go in and out of the water. Fur wouldn't. Luckily in Syracuse, I found some bright yellow clothe with black round spots and made numerous loin cloths for Russ and Frank which quite surprised the visitors from across the pond. They would wear them all day, day after day and all summer. The sun browned their bodies and bleached the cloth, so eventually they looked all one piece.

Towing two miles over to Parson's one day, I left the boys on the dock to dive and fool around in the water while I went to the farmhouse for milk. One the way back I met a woman coming up the grade who indignantly sputtered to me that there were two boys down at the dock jumping in the water in the nude and she had young girls at her cottage. To her surprise, I laughed out loud. "Come down with me," I said, "They are my boys. They are not nude, they had on faded 'Tarzan suits.'"

Another day, Russ, Frank and I were at the Parson's end of the pond. We had rowed over, taken the car, driven to Ellisburg, some thirteen miles away, stocked up on groceries and needed articles (often we bought for a week), and were ready to return to camp but during our grocery buying, a storm had come up from the south, and the pond was whipped into waves by the wind. I knew I *had* to return to the cottage somehow as Grandma Bryan and Aunt Minnie were there alone, and both along in years. I had the boys hold the boat while we got it loaded. I planned to skirt the shore – a longer way but wiser. I rowed and rowed that day, against the waves with the boat bobbing around and the boys ordered to spread out flat between the cartons. I did not know it, but a small group of people had begun to watch me with field glasses from the shore, anxious as to the outcome. With wearied arms, I pulled into an indentation of the pond at Blount's cottage where, thoroughly wet thru, we raced for the house, and found no one there. So all three of us crawled under the porch and sat shivering until the wind abated. Minnie and Gram did not seem unduly alarmed. Their motto was "Grace will manage, somehow." Their dependency on me however taxed a bit further my sense of responsibility to children and to them.

Janet at this time was in Syracuse with her Todey. She and my father and mother would arrive for the weekend and J. Russell would come walking out the shoreline with his wide open arms when he perceived me coming to meet him. We all loved the place except for, perhaps, some reservations on the part of my mother who tolerated a great deal because of our evident pleasure. I can see her sitting in the boat wearing dark glasses and carrying an umbrella outspread over her head, body as stiff as a ramrod and a pained expression on her face. She hated the water and was truly afraid of it. With so much of it around, we couldn't even get her to go wading. She loved to play croquet though and no one could beat her at it. In order to play at all, we had to cart the equipment at least an eighth of a mile to a section near the channel where the sand was flat and hard packed.

In September, as home-going neared, the breezes would send the drying leaves scurrying up the sandy shores, the gulls cry would become a longer wail and grayer, heavier clouds would pass majestically overhead. As if with a triumphal chord, all nature would burst into a colorful out-giving and fading go to sleep for its period of rest.

All valuables were carted home, window shutters were in place and the padlock was put on the door. In the earlier years, no one ever molested the place but later on it was broken into so many times we grew to expect it.

Back in Syracuse, school began again, work at the League returned and Sundays, the family ritual of dinners together, eight grownups and three children. I felt I owed my father, mother, Minnie and Gram a great deal for all the stepping-in to help they had carried thru for me, so a Sunday together was little enough to repay them. They all enjoyed it tremendously. There were a few times, however, when J. Russell wanted me just for himself so we'd get the three women to work and we'd slip away to have a dinner in Utica, Auburn, or some chosen place.

This recalls the sudden departures from home. J. Russell has a restless streak in him, which at times earlier in life than now, called for immediate action. I remember the day he came home and, without previous discussion, asked if I would be ready at eight o'clock in the morning. "What for?" I asked. "A trip," he answered. "Where?" I asked. "I don't know." "How long will we be gone?" "Oh, about two weeks." Not as used to this then as I became later, my mind raced thru the necessary preparations. Jan could stay with my mother and Minnie. She had to go to school anyway. Russ was about four and Frank, a lusty baby still tied to the necessity of bottles and diapers. "Two weeks!" I thought with dismay. Lucky I could get a substitute teacher for my work. I stayed up all night to pack, wash and dry diapers, prepare formula in advance, ice pack a carrying chest, ready the house for leaving but stood to stay with a grin at 8 A.M. – "I'm ready." It was a rather hectic two weeks with such small children. I do not recall where we went. We went on so many small trips (and longer ones) but I did respond joyously to the spontaneity of it.

About this time my father suffered a stroke. He had complained at times about how the constant fifty to one hundred miles a day driving was taking a great deal out of him. He wanted to give it up and return to a small drug store. He bought one in Hannibal, New York, and we found out he had dreams of running a small fruit farm nearby.

None of us foresaw the stroke. It robbed him of speech. He was sixty years old at the time. My loving father lost his ability to work on violins, to be a salesman and to talk. Strangely enough, though his thoughts would not work out into words, he could write them clearly on paper.

Gradually, a few words came back but things were never the same again. It was a blow to him, to all and especially to my mother.

Our musical grouping was again reduced in number. Now there were only my cello and my mother's piano. Janet was learning the violin. She had talent, it was obvious, but no inner drive to go ahead with it as Helen had.

With J. Russell's marvelous help at home with the children and also the help of the three older women, I was still working in the field of Adult Education in one capacity or another, part time or whole as conditions allowed. There were twenty three and a half years of this in the County – as Teacher, Assistant County Organizer, County Organizer, and when the C. V. E. E. B. (County Education & Extension Board) came into existence later, at times as County Supervisor and Assistant County Supervisor. Other girls named Helen Valentine, Esther Hefner, Fredricka Zeeb and Marian O'Neil were in the picture.

In Albany, Miss Caroline A. Whipple was the head of the Adult Education Bureau. Occasionally she toured the state giving supervision, teaching methods and planning conferences. In 1931, she asked me to give a talk on Americanization in Onondaga County and Direct Method Teaching at a state conference at Morrisville College. I was petrified! I liked all of the work tremendously but not speech making. Once all those eyes turned upon me, my self-consciousness, which had plagued my childhood school days, would return and my mind became incapable of giving out anything I knew. So this confrontation was particularly dreaded, together with the knowledge that Miss Whipple didn't know anything about my inabilities as a speaker. I inwardly appealed to the silent guardians for help as it was a two-day conference.

175

The way it came was unexpected and undreamed of. I left the two boys with their Dad and Jan came to stay at Todey's for the night. On the morning of June 21st, the session opened and dignitaries addressed the meeting. Miss Whipple, I knew, was expecting me to give those attending an interesting and shining account of actual work being accomplished in Onondaga County which had been the pioneer project and a great deal connected with this newer field (Adult Education) of endeavor. I was growing uneasy and actually frightened as eleven o'clock neared when mine was to become the keynote speech. At five minutes to eleven, an attendant came to me and whispered in my ear, "You are wanted outside in the hallway." Miss Whipple looked up and seemed disturbed that I was called just as she was going to introduce me. The attendant went to her and whispered something in her ear. She looked startled but said nothing to me.

As I opened the door into the hall, there stood J. Russell and the two boys. I expected the unexpected of J. R. but this seemed the ultra of unexpectedness. Russell was smiling as was usual in the face of all things good, bad or indifferent. "You have to come home," he said, "Your mother needs you." Still I was puzzled. Quietly he said, "Your mother found your father dead in bed beside her when she awoke this morning. Come on, they'll take it from here." A second stroke had taken my father's body from his further use. For several days, I felt his presence in the house. Theosophy had given mental acceptance of this passing as a thing of beauty not of tragedy but the spirit had still to accept the seeming separation of persons. Living went on.

I now insert some more about Janet. First about 1925, one day I returned from downtown to find the house and yard full of children dressed in their best, playing games and running in and out in noisy glee. Astonished, I asked Mrs. Conner who they all were. She said Janet said she was having a party. Then asking Janet, found she had wanted a party, had sent invitations home by the children in her grade in school (early June) and all had arrived. I started to admonish but did a right face, went down the street and purchased what we needed in ice cream, cookies and candy and a big party we had. Later asking Jan about, "How come?" she replied, "Oh, you're always so busy. I wanted a party. I made up my mind I could manage. It was lucky for me that you came home in time to get the 'eats' though." The children were all from about the third grade.

At an even earlier age, I ran into the problem of temper tantrums with her (she won't want to read this). Determined I'd conquer that, before it ever started, I filled the bath tub half full of water, picked her up screaming, kicking self, and dumped her in clothes, shoes and all. She was so astonished, she looked up at me with big eyes, all fight gone and finally slowly grinned. There was no more trouble that way until a few years later. Then she decided she just wasn't going to school. She was bigger. I couldn't handle her. I asked Russell to help me. At first he refused, as he never had interfered before. I insisted. So Jan was picked up around the waist and kicking, biting and screaming driven to school. I did not go along. "What did you do with her?" I asked. He responded, "I just put her in the principal's office, told the principal she'd refused to come to school, and walked out." It was *finis* then - never another temper spell. She showed evidence she deeply respected J. Russell for it.

I can see her now trailing grownup's clothes and stamping along in high heels sometimes playing "Mama" to Frank, who was ten years younger, as she wheeled him in his carriage. There were innumerable tea parties in the back yard under the peach tree near the garage, attic dress-ups when it rained. In winter, with the boys there were fights, snow forts, snow tunnels and riding down the hill across the road on sleds. The last I would watch with some anxiety as the sleds could have carried them into busy Westcott Street. There were the usual accidents associated with children, neighbor's windows broken by balls, wrecked trellises when the youngsters thought they could climb them, etc. J. R. and I weathered all. J. Russell loved children and understood their viewpoint. Find out what was in their minds before you punish, he'd say. Perhaps it was a youthful error in judgment, not deliberate action. I adored his fairness. I could take it all, but the quarreling. Then I'd silently and quietly by observation determine who was the instigator or who should be sent to a room alone - perhaps both of the boys or Jan. Half an hour later, the door would open, a head would come out, "I'm ready to be good now." I would say O. K. and peace would reign.

Calm action to calm. It worked. Not being perfect sometimes, I'd storm about it. The boys were greatly given to teasing each other, usually when their busy heads had nothing to occupy them for a time. Frank was more adept at this than Russ, though all three were at times guilty. They meant no real harm. Just a desire to stir up action. Dad said it was like growing pains, "necessary but not greatly enjoyed." He would suggest a game of catch with them and this positive turn would do the trick. I told J. R.

178

he should have had a dozen and I believed it. I learned a great deal from his attitude.

Coming down from camp one day, the day was hot and the three were tired from boat handling and packing the car to return to Syracuse. A wrangle started. I was tired too. "This is going to stop," I determined. So I drove off the side of the road, stopped the car, and didn't say a word. After a few minutes, someone came to in the back seat and asked, "What are we stopping for?" "Oh!" I said, "I'm waiting for you to get thru quarreling, so I can drive." No amount of hollering or scolding would have had the same immediate effect. I give them credit – all three, if they understood *why* you were making a point about anything, would cooperate. I thought I had three pretty swell people.

"Daddy Russell" gave me ideas many times on how to handle boys especially. One day when Russ was not yet four, the neighbor two doors away were having a new garage put up. The framework was up with 2 x 4's spaced upward to the ridgepole. Looking out of the kitchen window, I saw little Russ sitting high up there on the ridgepole dangling his feet into the spaces. I rushed out the door, I suppose ready to holler – anyway frightened. J. Russell grabbed me, "Don't say a word!" he said. He walked over slowly and talked to Russ, asked him how it was up there and if it was fun. Russ grinned and, under his dad's direction, slid down to the lower levels and into his father's arms. Weak-kneed, I sat down on the steps. Russ was afraid of *nothing* and later Frank imitated him in all he tried. They were a great pair. With Jan there were girl friends, campfire activities, Tully Lake camping, rollerskating, dancing, spit curls, teenage exaggerated styles and all the dreams of young girls up to and thru high school graduation.

With the boys the football days came. One afternoon, the ball was accidentally kicked into a neighbor's garage window. Irate and storming, the man appeared at the door stating his case in no uncertain tones. "I'm certain they didn't mean to do it," I stood up for them with conviction, "They'll be over with a broom to sweep up the glass and if you'll help them remove the window frame they will carry it to the hardware store and have the glass replaced." "Well, I'll be damned," he said, and went away grinning. Frank being three years younger than Russ may not remember this but Russ would. Frank seemed to come in for his share of cuts and bruises. Frank was at the receiving end of a toy thrown by Russ, his forehead cut. Frank stepped on sharp clam shells at camp and had to go on crutches nearly all one summer to keep the sand out of his foot. If it wasn't one thing, it was another *with both boys.*

For some time the Conner's upstairs had been having increasing financial difficulties. Charlie Conner was an engraver and business was poor. Month after month they got further behind in the rent. The relations were so excellent between the two families that J. Russell accepted the Conner notes in lieu of rent due. But the doing of this made it increasingly difficult for us to meet the rather high mortgage payments and interest, until it became evident something would have to be done. The previous owner holding the mortgage did not wish to decrease the amount of payment nor wait too long. After carefully thinking it over, we decided if nothing could be done it would have to revert and all payments to date we would *mentally* consider as *rent* paid. That left us with a decision – what do we do now? By rearrangement of finances, perhaps we could manage a down payment on a single house, it was thought. We looked and looked. They were either too expensive for our means or too far from the store or the school. Frank was five, Russ was eight and Jan was fifteen. We found a house on Demong Road and were to have signed papers for it in the afternoon. At noon, a friend in the bank called J. Russell and said, "Russ, weren't you looking for a house? The bank is taking one over at 935 Comstock Avenue. Fellow is going to lose one mortgage on it and it can be purchased cheap for the other. Interested?" J. Russell phoned me. We hurried right over at noon and looked at the house. The bank official met us and showed us through. It was nearly all rented to college students which gave us he clinching idea that we could finance it. So that very afternoon it was purchased and we went back to 710 Westcott Street breathless with our good fortune.

Today, May 1st, 1967, J. Russell asked me, "How many years have we lived here?" "Thirty-five this July," I answered, "And in two days we will have been married forty-four years." He responded, "I don't believe it. Four and four is eight years." Sounds characteristic! Sitting here with a broken left arm, I have been writing on this story of "me" for all day. "Shame on you for such absorption in yourself!" I think. To which I answer, "I won't be ashamed! I didn't start this long dissertation myself."

For years we used the house of five bedrooms and attic for student rooms and dorm and kept enough for us but it was a full house and an interesting one. We had some fine boys (all but one), mostly from Forestry College. The income kept the house going so my work was for the education of our three, or so I thought. The downstairs rooms were of excellent size for family dinners, for meetings, entertaining, and special occasions and so they were used.

At camp, John Cimbal, his brother and others pitched a tent not far from our cottage. John taught the boys and Janet to swim. John and the boys sometimes shot paper wads at the camp occupants from the loft over the porch. John came often to the pump to secure his "iron" from the well. The boys adored him. We all thought and think a lot of John. One summer it was John and his new wife Amelia (Mickey) and still later a young John added. Mickey was and is remarkable. When John was working in Syracuse, she and little John would await his return. We saw them often in the tent on the sand peninsula but not as often as we might have if I hadn't been truly afraid of their more than excellent watch dog, trained to act on command. He would have let no one anywhere near the tent. Mickey loved the outdoors or she wouldn't have been content to stay there. At times we sat on logs and sketched waves, driftwood or gulls. Aunt Minnie joined in this pastime. Mickey could handle a boat as well as John. They caught loads of perch and bullheads and occasionally larger great northern pike.

One summer Russ, of his own accord, went to Greenpoint to work for the Sawyer's handling the boats for the early fishermen. With the money he earned, he bought us an Evinrude Motor for our rowboat. After that, we parked the car at the point for years. Crossing to camp was closer coming from Sawyer's but when there were too many for the boat, the Parson's stop was first made by car. I can see Russ in that boat, a-straddle the front with legs overside shooting thru the pond, steering the motor from that positive by a rigged up contrivance of his own, often with Tarzan yells, crow calling or outbursts of noisy song. Again, I reiterate, he was afraid of nothing. No wonder he dreamed of being a flyer. At the same tie his thoughts were for others and I never knew him to be truly reckless. He had full command of any situation, even when quite young.

Frank brought Charlie Sheridan to camp for a few days. Bill Wheeler had left a kayak of his in the loft of the camp. These two got it down one day and, forgetting to inform us of their intent or perhaps not really having any definite plan at all, paddled two miles to Parson's and then, tired out, lay in the grass on shore talking while they rested. Hunting for them, I found the kayak gone and nothing in sight anywhere, my concern mounting as time went on. I finally started walking the two miles to Parson's to get help or hire a motorboat, but found the boys there talking happily. They were really too young (perhaps 8 or 9), and especially without anyone knowing, to have gone that distance on a pond subject to occasional storms. I was not at all happy about that.

Another time *I was really concerned.* It was necessary to leave my mother and Grandma Bryan (around 80) at camp for awhile, while I carried out some necessary business in the city. While I was away, Grandma Bryan felt called upon to fill up the can containing kerosene which was used to light the Coleman Stove but she filled it with gasoline. When my mother went to prepare food, the stove and can burst into flames, the curtains got on fire, and the inside walls were blackened. The boys raced in and out frantically with pans of sand. They got it out, but I returned to a stove full of sand, and tables, chairs, floor and foodstuffs covered. I was grateful that the cottage still stood, but what a mess!

I've been talking of disturbing things! In all the happy days, occasionally the lake storms would come. When they came in the daytime, I'd love to watch the black clouds scudding the sky and the waves answer to their anger racing shoreward in increasing fury as the wind increased. This could give deep response to pleasure and I'd feel swung out into the music of McDowell's Poem. I loved the wildness. But if those same storms came at night when I was in charge of sleeping older women and children, and no one but me to do for them, then as the cottage trembled in the wind, I would get dressed to stand ready. As the lightning played weird fantasies thru the cracks in the siding, with the sea roaring its noisy protests; the wind howling and the thunder smashing and growing across the sky; I'd feel like the keeper of a lonely lighthouse standing high to the sea, the rocks of faith only holding back the demon waters from their angry lashings at me and mine. But morning would come at last, and with it sunrises more beautiful than ever in their fresh washed air and invigorating coolness.

There were the shorter timed storms but some came each summer which we called the three day ones. These are particularly remembered. The wind blew hard, the air turned cold, the skies were gray and threatening, the waters so strong that no boat could be launched from the dock nor safe except in strong hands. Then we were truly tied to the camp for three days of sand-blowing winds. To get water from the pump was really a chore. On one of these occasions, a rowboat washed in. An elderly fisherman couldn't get back to the mainland. We took him in. There was no way to reach his family until the storm abated. On the third day, a big Coast Guard boat docked at our pier. The boys ran down to it. The Coast Guard wanted to know had we seen an elderly man fishing in a boat now gone for three days? Yes! He'd been with us three days. We'd cared for him. The Coast Guard took him back to his family and his folks came later for the boat. They had not expected to find him alive.

On another occasion, the Conner family was with us. There were five young men tenting near the channel. They had traveled (up until the time of the storm) across to Ackerman's for food and water. Stranded, they came to us for water. On the second or third time, we discovered they had had nothing to eat since the previous day. Their provisions were gone. At camp, a similar situation existed. We had let supplies run down purposely for camp was to be closed that weekend for the summer. Somehow we found we had an over-supply of pancake flour and several boxes of brown sugar. Florence helped prepare the food. The number of pancakes those boys ate astonished Florence. I can hear her merry laugh as she would retell it later. they disappeared with the end of the storm, saying, "Never would they try that place again." But these are really the exceptions to days and days of sun and beautiful weather. The big lake too would rest sometimes in two or three days in utter calm so glassily shining that one could imagine walking upon it without sinking in.

In the last of June and early July, the shores would be covered with the terrible-smelling dead "Moon Eyes." Then all went to the water's edge armed with rakes, shovels and baskets. For more than our frontage we cleaned the beach each day, gathered up the fish, dug holes further away, and buried them. The vacationers would exclaim, "What a beautiful beach! Let's camp right here." Sometimes we'd have to shove them off our property. The idea persisted that the whole peninsula was state property free to everyone. The argumentative ones we invited to pay our taxes for us and then named the owners of the land parcels thru from the channel to Parson's mainland road. Of course, the state claims so many feet from the water's edge inland. We allowed for that. The edge changed from year to year and from spring to fall of each year. Where was the edge? Where it was at the moment of asking.

Janet's interest in boys had been developing and their interest in her. Bill Wheeler was around camp a great deal. But at home one evening she brought in a new young man, Howard W. Wells. Intuitively I felt this is it. She had had one year in college in Home Economics. Jan was never the dedicated student. Another avenue of endeavor awaited her. At length they spoke of marriage. I'd been married at nineteen years old. What could I say to her?

So the prettiest wedding that could be devised was arranged for them on September 4, 1937, here at 935 Comstock Avenue. Her brothers in their white trousers and white shoes and dark jackets attended her. They looked adorable I thought, nine and twelve in age. The house was crowded with people. The weather was very warm and sunny. Refreshments were a buffet lunch in the dining room Even before the occasion was over the day turned cool. It seemed too early for it. Their trip took them into Canada and they said they nearly froze, being unprepared.

One thing was unusual about the wedding. On their return from Canada, they were to stay here at 935 Comstock and keep track of the boys and the three roomers we had, while Dad and I took off for a trip to Europe on an American Legion Pilgrimage. We said laughingly that they got married and we took the trip. The store was left in charge of capable Paul Galloway. I arranged to be away from the League.

Again, I make the decision not to write here the whole story as it is as at least partially written elsewhere. A very few anecdotes will suffice. The French Government wanted to give the Legionnaires a pilgrimage to Paris for half price on everything. Thousands took advantage of it, taking their wives along at the reduced rate. We landed at Cherbourg and proceeded to Paris to find the hotel equipped with a big ballroom filled with double beds for married couples. An amused roar went up at that. No privacy, not even screens! The management was quite disturbed that after all that work, we noisy Americans found other hotels.

Paris held a special evening for the Americans in a tremendous hall and with impressive ceremonies. Thousand of Legionnaires were presented with a huge bottle of cognac, twenty to twenty-seven inches tall. Neither J. R. or I were used to liquors, so he said, "What will we do with it? We can't carry it across Europe!" So on our way back to the hotel, we gave it to the cab driver whose look of elation and astonishment can still be recalled.

I'll add a few episodes out of many.

As we passed by train from Germany toward Austria, a young Chinese lad who'd been studying in England sat in the double seat with us. We were happily visiting. The large burly German conductor came thru the train and ordered the young man out of the seat to give it to another passenger who had just come on the train. J. Russell stood up defiantly and said, "Nein, Nein, Er ist mein freund." The conductor left. But shortly the train stopped. Out of all that car in the train, only J. Russell and the Chinese lad were ordered out of the car. As times were of uncertain feelings for Americans, I sat bewildered. No explanation was given. Time passed. Neither returned. I had visions of attempting to find an American Consul and leaving the train which unaccountably started to move and kept on going for some twenty minutes when it again stopped. It was now dark outside and I was frankly apprehensive. After a fifteen minute stop we again started moving backward in the direction we had come from and then stopped again. I looked in vain for some explanation but in the train car, all sat unconcerned in Germanic placidity. Suddenly the two returned. After a grueling forty-five minutes, I found that nearing the border, they had had to declare all the money on their persons and any traveler's checks. The train meantime had been switching to another track!

Later we arrived in Salzburg, Austria, without reservations. J. Russell left me in the depot while he hunted accommodations. A trinket and view cards on the counter led me to purchase them. Some American money received American change. I did not realize at the moment that that change would become so important. It was Saturday and all banks and changers were closed until Monday, but having it allowed our going up a very high mountain in the Austrian Alps by cable car and later eating in a Swiss Chalet.

Another time I was left sitting by our baggage in the depot. One arrives on the edge of Venice by train. It was 11 P. M. We had no reservations for a hotel, so again Russell left me and went by gondola to find a place to stay. He was gone and gone. Every few minutes, a nicely dressed young Italian man would appear, approach me and say, "Albergo?" Not knowing what it meant, I felt a shake of the head to say "no" was the safe answer. My sitting there in the middle of the night alone must have puzzled him. At last J. R. returned. We had a fine place, not at all a tourist hotel but quaintly delightful. Enthused by the moonlight and the gondola ride, J. R. said, "Let's leave our things and go out on the Grand Canal." It was a thrilling experience! The red-sashed gondolier suddenly burst into Grand Opera and we felt in as unreal a world as a stage setting, with the moonlight subduing many bright colors, with the lapping of the waters and the deep-chested singing. We stopped at St. Mark's Square, fed the pigeons, wandered in the cathedral and were two very happy people without a care in the world. Finally around 3 A. M. we returned to the hotel to find the gate in the iron fence surrounding the premises locked and the hotel unlighted. After our lengthy pounding on the gate, the irate proprietor appeared in a long, white night shirt and a stocking cap of white muslin, which had a tasseled end that reached down his back to below his knees. He looked so funny, we had to repress laughter, but his expression said, "Those crazy Americans." I looked up at the sign in front of the hotel. It said, "Albergo."

An exceedingly funny episode happened at lunchtime, when we found we understood not a thing on the menu and no one, guest or personnel, understood English. One by one they trained to understand us, our halting German and meager French. The waiter brought the cook from the kitchen, then the manager's wife, then the manager, and all tried. We pointed to another couple's dinner. Russell said, "Etwas fish." It seemed to mean something so we waited. Finally in came hot chocolat, and an enormous platter of fish, from tiny ones to seafood and an enormous single fish in the middle. Suddenly we were laughing. The merriment grew. Soon everyone in the dining room, the waiter, the cook with his elaborate headgear, the manager's wife, the manager and the Paine's were laughing so hard that the tears ran down our faces and I know I would have slid under the table from weakness if it had gone on much longer. That mountain of assorted fish on that huge platter was amazing.

I wish I could tell all the episodes from that trip in this "book"

After three months of wandering around Europe, we returned home on a cruise boat stopping in Greece, Yugoslavia, Sardinia, Algiers, Gibralter and the Azores. As J. Russell was sea sick in his cabin on most of the journey, it caused some of the passengers to exclaim, "We thought you were fooling when you mentioned your husband as being on board." At the time, he was standing wanly and thin near the ship railing and towering behind him was the Statue of Liberty.

Once home again, the duties of house; caring for the rooms occupied by the Forestry students; the night school teaching; the boys now twelve and nine; and the weekend family dinners were recommenced. Jan and Howie had moved into small quarters on East Genesee Street, which proved very unsatisfactory. In time, Bob was born and I was in their apartment on Strong Avenue when he took his first steps. The busy world was full of memories.

My social life was almost non-existent. There was the Women of Rotary for occasional dinners at the Onondaga Hotel and sewing meetings at homes. This membership had started early in my married life and only recently was discontinued. I do not recall just when I joined the Onaway Club which is a literary one in which the members write papers on countries in the world, states in the United States, books, events, notable people, and the like. These were given at the meetings and often there were pictures, views, and maps to add interest. The members were elected officers. At one time, I was President. Delta Gamma Alumnae doings faded for me as younger girls came to take the place of those whom I had known. For many years, I had belonged to the Poetry Club of Syracuse, trying my hand in this direction. I suppose I should put in here a few of my efforts. This really is for the family. Omit reading if you like.

> Nature holds the key within
> Mutely speaking noble truth -
> Cyclic changes with the season
> The earthly lives of man complete
> A hidden time in subtler form
> A return again to infancy,
> As tender leaves upon a stem
> Return again at Springtime's whisper.
>
> To us
> The world's a mirror
> The mirror of a passing show
> Brief glances gaining as we live
> Brief glimpse into the dark unknown

Behind the mirrored image
Beyond the passing show
We lightly touch with vibrant living
Extensions of the world of sense
Our eyes mistake the temporal marching
Too briefly glimpsing dark unknown.

To us
The world's a mirror
The mirror of the passing show.
Outside the prison of ourselves
Vibrations rise to laws unsought.
We see, not blinded by our eyes
We hear, not deafened by our ears
When we
Step behind the mirror
The mirror of the passing show.

I know because I know
Sometimes not by thought or reason
I know because I know
With definite certainty
I know because I know
Its source obscurely hidden
I know because I know
Some call it Intuition.

Because you understand so well
The emotional suffering of another
The suppressed Being welling up with that keen
desire
For companionship, life and love.
Because you understand
You silent are and quiet
But with deep and tendr'st feeling
Send loving thoughts – knowing well

That time has its ways mysterious
And out of blank and weary ruts
We find ourselves rich in life
When Time is right.

Repression's for the man of Instinct
Thru it Will, Control, he may be taught.
But let him pass, however far
Into the realms of reason and of thought
'Tis then expression gains him freedom
Backed by Will, Control, from his own Being.
Until good judgment or adversity
Gains him differentiation.
Then thru knowledge first hand of laws
So few, and only Godly
(Given Men as guideposts to a Master)
He transgresses not, except deliberately
And suffers doubly in his Soul
From earthly causing and effect.

Mabel Burlingham and I were close friends. We often
rode in the car to a beautiful place, parked and settled down
for a tremendous uplift by reading together highly sensitive
and inspiring writings on mysticism, philosophy, and inner
awareness of things of higher than the ordinary run of daily
experiencing. Some examples of these were Kahlil Gibran;
A. E.; Claude Bragdon; Martin Buber and Krishnamurit
and others. Later Luelle Nitschke joined us and out of
these beginnings of three, there developed a day class in
discussions of Theosophy, Mysticism, Comparative
Religion, Archeological Discoveries, and topics of interest

to those present including Spiritualism, The Essenes, the Popul Vuh, etc. I am carrying this still in 1968, meeting every two weeks when that is possible. At these meetings, at times, I had distinct feelings that I was being spoken thru, not speaking myself. A few of any who read this will understand my reference. Brought up short, I would think, "I didn't know that I knew that."

Along this line, on one occasion, a friend of mine invited me to a party. I was a stranger there to all but two, the hostess and Mrs. A. E. Johnson, wife of the English professor at Syracuse University. All the rest had known each other for some time. The hostess asked me *for fun* if I would come dressed as a gypsy and pretend to read fortunes for entertainment. I dressed in an appropriate costume and entered into the spirit of the occasion with hilarity. I will make up something about each one, I thought, as a gypsy would. But a change of focus of attention was inborn upon me and the group found me reading each character with vivid clarity, and giving answers to personal problems I knew nothing about. The atmosphere in the room grew electric and intense. Hilarity changed to surprised and awed astonishment. Suddenly I felt as if told, "Stop! You are getting beyond their depth." I came away from the party baffled and deeply stirred, puzzling over it for days. The question of the wisdom of allowing the dominance of another consciousness to talk thru me was deeply questioned. I decided I wanted none of it. There were other instances which deepened this decision.

The moving out of the consciousness from the body as we do quite normally each night in sleep (and permanently in death) *can* bring some daytime experiences which have been written of many times in discerning literature. On one vividly-remembered occasion, happening as I came into the dining room at home after reading some very beautiful, uplifting material, I suddenly experienced an almost transfiguring emotion of the sensing of beauty, but this was a deeper version – a kind of sensing of the *essence* of beauty – an experience hard to describe; but was a colored splendor which gathered all life into a glorious, pulsating unity. Words are lacking to describe this tremendous height of cosmic awareness. Only twice in my life has anything so tremendous occurred! The second, coming after a deeply absorbing morning meditation. I have heard people say about themselves, "I was carried away, out of myself." I believe this is a form of this experience.

But I am quite the ordinary person in interests, occupation and desires. The experiences described throughout, sent me into research toward explanation and I'm still at it. There seems to be in man areas which have yet to be understood. They are quite normal. There is nothing of the psychotic about them. As I had grown up, I had discovered that some people seemed to lack the "knowing" and some others had it rarely or occasionally. During the years, I have known a *very* few who had it quite completely and under the control of their will. One just doesn't know why E. S. P. and subconscious (or shall I say superconscious) knowledge emerge in the same person in different ways, in directness or in symbols; nor what brings them on occasion and not in others; nor why a "knowing" *prior* to an event can be, without it meaning ordered destiny; nor why one can discuss all these things so freely and without restraint with some people and clam up so completely with others. But switches of consciousness *may* be experienced by more people than is commonly realized, because they prefer *not* to mention it. To what great depths must we plumb to fulfill the admonition "KNOW THYSELF."

At Mabel Burlingham's an evening literary group met with Professor Yerlington, an English Professor at S. U., as leader. He had a searching mind and an Emersonian outlook. These were soul-satisfying evenings of great richness. This group continued on for many years until Mabel became ill and went to live with a daughter in Massachusetts.

My daughter and I continued to play it telepathically. Often we would arrive at the phone at the same time. There were numerous incidents. I will choose one. Jan was expecting me to come to her house for the day. I left home and had driven perhaps five miles when I got a mental picture of her house, closed up, with house and yard empty. I was about to turn around and go back wondering what had happened. But as the day was beautiful and I love to drive, went on thinking, "I'll prove it out." The mental picture was right. All was empty. Later in the day, Jan called, "Mother, I am sorry. Howie was going out of town on an errand in the early morning. Suddenly he said, 'Why don't you go with me?' I had to race so fast to get dressed and ready, that I forgot to call you and later on the way tried to tell you mentally."

The work at the Americanization League in the Onondaga County area continued, either in a full-time or part-time capacity and I taught a Saturday morning class of the foreign born who were preparing for citizenship, either in the Y. M. C. A. or in the League office, with the summer school vacations for the boys spent at Lake Ontario at the camp.

PART V

One cannot begin to relate all the experiences of a lifetime nor explain all the lessons coming thru them, but looking backward one can see the "moving finger on the wall," the movement of destiny and Divine planning. The richness of experiencing is soul satisfying. A friend of mine once said, "Some people live several lives in one lifetime." I'm inclined to think that can be true.

Chapter 10

We were seated at the table in the Sandy Pond Cottage, Grandma Bryan, Aunt Minnie and I. The boys and Janet were there or nearby outside. The battery radio was on. Suddenly the news came over the set and suddenly, I *knew* that this was that something for which I had been bracing myself inwardly. The enormity of it flooded my being. I rose up wildly and said, "This is it!" and then down went my head on the table with tears welling up. The remoteness of the place we were in, the gentle lapping of the waves; the sunny sand; the happy repose all disappeared in a sensing of blackness, of terrific world turmoil and sadness. Everything changed within and without. I *knew* that terrible upheaval would affect everyone including that small circle in the cabin. Grandma Bryan looked at me uncomprehendingly and said in characteristic "Pollyanna" cheerfulness, "It can't hurt us!" I don't know but I think I must have glared at her. "But it will!" I said and *knew* something indefinite, indefinable but overwhelming was coming.

I dashed out of the cottage and down the hill to the pond and sat for some time with my head on my hands to still that inner turmoil. The news was to affect us all individually! I felt weak and trembly until the awareness of the pond returned, the tall grasses by my feet, the fishermen going by in boats. Nothing seemed really changed – just unaware. The birds sang in the trees; the gulls called across the sky; our boat was moored near my feet; a bullfrog croaked; the water murmured quietly. Nature was undisturbed. Man only was out of step. I took the walk thru the trees to the "bay" and, turning, passed the sand hills to Lake Ontario. How undisturbed it was, stretching out to infinity. The sky came down to meet it way out there. It seemed to say, "Infinite time, infinite changes. When you see narrowly you cannot see the whole." It was as if a hand was laid upon my shoulder.

It was late summer. Very soon we were to return to Syracuse and the duties awaiting us. The college students at the house would be returning. Russell (III) was in college in Engineering. He was doing well. He was nearly 17 years old. The newspapers were full of the draft. All the boys in the house were alarmed and disturbed seeing the break in their college years and in their future plans. The waves of patriotism increased. Some wanted to jump into it with both feet to stop this would-be madness; some to protect their families in the U. S. – as it was strongly talked that Japan would attack us next. Alarm, dismay, and reaction stirred all hearts. The number of uniforms on the streets increased.

My work took me on trains and buses. They were filled to capacity. The younger folks were moving out to camps, to duty, to cross seas. I longed with all my heart to be at home in all this turmoil but found myself plodding along with the work for the state as I was still working in the State Department of Adult Education under the leadership of Miss Whipple. I helped organize classes for those who desired citizenship in my fifteen counties, talking with superintendents and officials in the Immigration and Naturalization Service, attending meetings and conferences and going to Albany and back at least once a week to staff meetings. Weekends at home, I caught up on the washing, the ironing, the cleaning and my family and student roomers' needs. I felt I was neglecting my family. It hurt deeply but I felt caught up in all the turmoil. My mother complained she never saw me any more. I felt it was fortunate that Theosophy was taking her attention and her energies.

J. Russell continued at the store at 252 West Washington Street at Syracuse Victory Soap Corp., with the help of Paul Galloway who became as a third son as the years went by. I can see J. Russell in my mind's eye as he stood at the door of the store with a big smile on his face. He was and is the friend of everyone who is in need of help. His philosophy of life seemed to come from his mother's attitude. Everything was fine always. It if wasn't, it did not exist for him. He shut it out completely. It "sparked" the "underdog," the numerous "down-on-their-luck'ers" who came in to obtain small items to sell from door to door. They responded to his attitude to the point of many saying J. R. was the best friend they ever had, and they meant it! The store often saw those released from jail, dopers, unemployed, homeless, derelicts, etc. They came in for sympathy. He gave them none. He wouldn't listen to stories or excuses. He told them all things like, "That was in the past!... Stand up and be a man... You can do it! ... It's in you!" I really think it did straighten some shoulders – if not all perhaps permanently. These were only small parts of the customers, of course. I responded deeply to this characteristic of his. It fitted in with my regard for all nationalities, colors and races with whom I had been working since 1917.

Young Russ was nearing the draft call. He felt he would rather enlist than be drafted. He also wanted to try for the Air Corps. His dad was very proud of him. I could only feel sadness in my heart. His exuberant, out-going spirit, his fun, his extreme youth, I saw them all, but to him it looked like adventure and adventure was part of his life's outlook. Little did he know, I thought, about the awfulness of war, but I trained myself to silence facing the seeming inevitable. There were moments, I know, when the state job, the house, the students, the boys, Janet's little family, J. Russell, Grandma B., Todey and Aunt Minnie, the many problems, the pulls on the heart strings, seemed more than I could take, but I schooled myself to carry on. At moments, I felt near the breaking point. There seemed no rest anywhere. There were the weekly Sunday dinners to get for the three older women and the family. I was so completely exhausted that sometimes I wished someone would wait on me, but I do not think anyone ever realized. J. Russell never guessed nor did I let him.

The family meal was an institution, a happy affair at Westcott Street or at Comstock Avenue. It started after Mr. Bryan's death and continued thru to 1945, some eighteen years, except when J. Russell and I were off on a vacation or a trip but those came later. Do not mistake me, I also welcomed these dinners. I felt that here was where I really belonged – with my family; but that I was caught in a closed situation that couldn't readily be changed.

Russ enlisted and continued in college until he was called. He and one of his best friends, Art Howe, also age

204

seventeen, were sworn in at the old Armory. They were two of a long line of young men lined up across the floor facing the officials. Russ had on a white, turtle-necked sweater. I can see it still. J. Russell and I sat in the balcony. Sensing how I felt, he turned to me and said, "Now, don't you dare cry!" "I won't," I said. "Send him into his decision happily," he whispered. I responded, "I will."

There were short patriotic speeches. The young men stood at attention, straight shoulders, no hesitation. Suddenly, again as in other times, I *knew*. I burst into crying. Reprovingly J. Russell said, "You said you wouldn't." All I could say was, "But he's going to be hurt – terribly hurt. I can't stand it." "Don't talk that way! He'll be all right – smile!!!" Roy Scroxton and his wife and the two of us met outside on the sidewalk. Their son was in the line too. She was crying; but I was in command again. Russ, Art and the Scroxton boy came by. J. Russell Sr. put his arm around me and whispered, "Good girl." The boys looked excited and happy. The big adventure had started. I kept up until they were no longer with us.

I don't want to go into the events of the Second World War. Much of the time I even shut it out of mind as something I did not want to know about, something unreal. Russ went into training – to Biloxi, Mississippi; to Toledo, Ohio; Phoenix, Arizona; Santa Ana, California; and to Stockton near Sacramento, California. I think on the whole his training was a happy experience. He received more college training in Toledo, Ohio. He met a lovely girl there who came to our home later, Thays Dow.

A time came when I longed so to see him that Frank and I went by train to Toledo and spent the day. We saw the training grounds. We met some of his friends. It was terribly hot and I was extremely uncomfortable with blisters I'd acquired from walking, but I didn't let him know. It was a real occasion for Frank and one I thoroughly enjoyed with him and Russell. I did not meet Thays then but heard of her. I did meet the Bersani boy whose family had entertained Russ one weekend at their home and Bob Parker and a Peterson lad. All these went thru the same training and all hoped to become pilots. Russ and Bob Parker won their wings. Art Howe became a navigator. Art Howe was a blond. Russ' hair was darkening. Art was quiet and enjoyed Russ who was very outgoing. Art lived just off Euclid Avenue on Huston Avenue. Bob Parker's family had a cottage at Sandy Pond at Ackerman's. We had not known this at the time as our camp was across the pond two miles away, on the lakeside shore. Time went on and so did the training. Art Howe finally left the group and went to Florida and then across the seas to the Eastern area.

Russ finally went to Camp Stockton near Sacramento. Then came the first real furlough. Bob Parker and he returned to Syracuse. We tried to get their furlough time extended by going to the local office and by telegrams but it couldn't be done. Bob went on the Lacona, New York, with his family. At home there was such a happy reunion. Excitement ran high, we had big dinners, took pictures in the front yard and all was so gay! Time was short! The Parker's and the Paine's met at the New York Central Railroad Depot. We were not to be allowed thru the gate so the boys said their goodbyes all around. As Russ got as far as the ticket gate, he suddenly turned to me and said again, "Goodbye, Mom," with such deep feeling that I caught it strongly. "Goodbye, Son," I said. For years and years that scene haunted me and sometimes my dreams.

On August 4th, 1944, the phone rang early. I answered. A man from The Post Standard paper asked me to tell him about my son Russell. As I started to talk, I sensed some confusion at the other end of the line. Suddenly he asked, "You haven't had a telegram?" "What telegram?" I asked. "There has been an accident," he replied. "To Russ?" I asked alarmed, "Is he badly hurt?" The young man at the other end realized I didn't know and backed out nervously.

I sped up the stairs to J. Russell. "Russ has been hurt, badly hurt," I said. "He'll be all right," responded J. Russell with his usual optimism. In a few minutes, the doorbell rang. It was the message from the War Department, curt and to the point: Russ had been killed about 6:30 P. M. on August 3rd, my birthday. I woke Frank and broke the news and, upset at the news, called Jan. Jan was carrying Donnie at the time and Howie said I gave her an awful shock. I didn't hear about that until later.

I sat down in the living room with deep sobs. J. Russell and Frank, thoroughly disturbed, moved to my side. Frank knelt at my knee. Suddenly I thought, "I can't do this. I must stop. J. Russell and Frank both need my help." I jumped up and walked away. I should have put my arms around those two wonderful people but for the moment I was struggling for control. Control was all I thought of. I acquired too much I think for I didn't cry again outwardly. There developed a big ache inside which seemed to consume me. Outside I was the same as before but often withdrawn from participation. J. Russell kept telling me to smile. I did. It was often just for them and for the rest of the family.

It was to be ten days before the casket arrived from California. The accident had been near Sacramento, twelve miles outside of camp. As John R. Pettinen and J. R. Paine raised the plane into the air from the base they knew right away that something was not right. In order to avoid houses and people twelve miles from the base, they flew under wires (many of them) and pancaked the plane to the ground. We never knew who was flying it at the moment. Robert W. Gray – a man from Modoc, California – wrote us. The plane just missed his car. A Mr. Oby, a colored man, and he ran to the plane and pulled the boys out just before the flames enveloped it. Both had been killed. Their initials were the same: J. R. P. The date of their death: my birthday, 1944.

At the time of the funeral ten days later, the house at 935 Comstock Avenue was filled with people, as well as the yard outside. The officer from the local Air Force at Mattydale came to officiate. It was 90 degrees F. The man had not brought a podium for his speech. He sent the men back for it. The people waited in the heat. The casket, with flag draped, remained closed. Over it was a large picture of Russ sent to us by a photograph shop in Sacramento, one Russell had had taken for my birthday. He smiled at me from the picture all during those long minutes. The tributes to Russ were heartfelt and numerous. All the people whom I'd known came – friends, relatives, and some of my former pupils, also the members of the Poetry Club who had written beautiful tributes to Russ. The officer said he'd never been able to talk so fervently. He said he'd been caught up in the atmosphere in the house. The newspaper man asked me questions. I was radiant and glowing. He did not know what to make of it and said he'd never had such an experience before: "The mothers usually were so crushed." I longed to tell him but cut myself short. I knew he certainly would not understand. For I was still living in the radiance of a tremendous experience, one I couldn't speak of for years to anyone unless they would believe what I *knew* was a true experience.

On the third day after Russ' passing, I awoke at 4 A. M. I was not used to waking up in the night. I looked out the front window. It was still dark. The room seemed to grow brighter with a golden glow. Suddenly I felt drawn out of myself. I was both in the bed sitting up and outside of it standing looking back. The room filled with pulsing happiness and there at the foot of the bed stood Russ with a radiant smile on his face. No word was spoken that my ears heard but he said clearly and distinctly to my mind, "Accept this, Mom. It's all in the planning." And deep love streamed from him to me. As I looked there was a click in my head and I was back in bed again sitting up but thrilled beyond words. I leapt from bed and woke J. Russell in his room, crying, "Russell, Russ has been here." Inwardly I didn't expect him to believe me but strangely, he did but his voice broke. I was caught up in that wonderful glowing experience for days. It carried me thru the funeral and the days that followed fading as mundane things took over again. At the funeral I noticed some looking at me with questioning eyes. I radiated complete happiness. No wonder some could not understand. Some said later, "You didn't really believe that Russell was gone. You were in shock." Often I wanted to tell them. It had become too precious an experience! I do not know whether I took Frank and Janet into my confidence then or later.

Those days must have been difficult for dear Frank.
Frank was now sixteen years old. I felt keenly his wavering
about enlisting or waiting. He asked for Dad's and my
advice. Somehow, I just couldn't give it. "Too much," I said
to myself, "Too much. I can't take this too." I felt Frank's
very keen disappointment that his eyes kept him out of pilot
training. He had his heart and mind full of dreams about it.
He felt Russ' going keenly. He felt he should do his part.
Russ was gone. It was his turn. He enlisted. By this time
there were no enlistment ceremonies. He awaited orders.
He was ordered to Fayetteville, South Carolina, Fort
Bragg.

J. Russell realized that it would help me so
tremendously if we went to the base with Frank to see
where he would be, so I could see it in my mind. I knew
Dad wanted it too. Neither of us realized how Frank would
resent this and I think he thought we were still thinking too
much of his being a little boy and perhaps we did in a
measure. Anyway, when we arrived he cut us off sharply.
From then on he was on his own. He showed us this
unmistakably. Dad understood immediately. I did not. I
was quite unhappy for some time until J. Russell made me
see more clearly, Frank was quite self-contained. He did
not even try to explain himself. Torn by love for him, I was
being too much the mother but didn't realize it.

I made some other mistakes with Frank. I couldn't
always get his reactions to things. I loved him so deeply but
he seemed at times to throw off closeness or affection.
Perhaps I failed to know that he was growing up in his own
individual way. I think he suffered more by my working

outside the home than Russ did. I found out much later that he resented the stacked-up dishes in the kitchen left undone when I was desperately trying to get somewhere on time or catch a train or bus. Dad was wonderful always in his help but there was just too much for me to handle. If I had life to live over again, I would not work outside of home, not if I had children growing up. I thought my working, my saving of money, would put all three thru college. Dad's store would not supply enough. I was mistaken in my idea of helping them. Life played a joke on me. Jan married. Russ passed into another experience and Frank's army life helped him eventually to finish college and inspired him to go on to M. A. and Ph. D. degrees. But like all folks I could not see that far ahead. It amuses me now to think about it. Trying to knock myself out when I really didn't need to in the end.

Frank had some reactions to the "shots" he had been given and was in the base hospital. We were not aware of it for a while as he didn't write much. Finally all was going better and he also was taking courses which would be accredited later to college work. We drove down to see him and he no longer seemed the young son but very much a man. He seemed to enjoy our visit very much. He had a furlough in June 1945. I had written that his Grandmother Tobey had died on June 5th. He came on June 9th, and talked to Grandma Bryan that evening. She had been found by me in a coma the day before and after a doctor's visit was in bed. She old Frank that he could write more on a postal card than anyone she ever knew; that she was tired but wanted to have a long talk with him in the morning about what he was doing, and his activities.

In the early morning, J. Russell and Frank went over to 113 Trinity place. I wanted to finish a few things at the house. Julia Howland, J. R.'s adopted sister, was there helping. But Grandma died just before I arrived. There were two funerals at 935 Comstock, five days apart. A tough furlough for Frank. Frank was scheduled to go back. We all congregated at the depot. He moved up thru the train to a platform further ahead. Somehow I was way down the line. The train started to move. I ran as fast as I could and just managed to get there to say "Goodbye" when I stepped behind a pillar and the dam broke. Julia looked at me and said, "Why Grace!" Frank was gone. We had sensed before he left us that he might be leaving the country, but did not now when or where.

Then began the loneliest days J. Russell and I knew in all our married life. J. Russell bolstered me many a time when I faltered – but he was rocked too. I wrote Frank in Japan twice a week, I tried desperately not to let our loneliness enter the picture but I feel he knew anyway. I sent him cookies and Xmas boxes. He told me the cookies arrived broken and stale. It was impossible to know whether all the mail reached him. A system of numbering letters would have told him. I didn't think of it.

The house on Lancaster Avenue where Jan, Howie and the two boys lived was sold and there seemed no place for them to move to, as places to rent were scarce. We were all so numb that at first it did not even occur to us that they could move into "Todey's" flat with Aunt Minnie who was now alone. This was soon accomplished. After they were there a month, in July, Aunt Minnie asked me one day if I would go to the doctor's with her as she felt things were not right. Dr. Reifenstein examined her and then told her to go and get dressed. He talked to me privately and said not to let her know if I could help it. She had stomach cancer, he said, of the galloping kind. He gave her two to three months, that was all. As we left, Aunt Minnie asked me, "What did he say?" I said, "Some stomach trouble. He'll help you."

Jan was wonderful! She cared for our aunt day and night. Aunt Min grew thinner and thinner and more and more pain developed. I helped as much as I could but my job had to be kept going; my own home run. Frank was still in Japan, but now the war was over. He wanted to come home but the Army takes its time. Then one day I was given a tremendous number of letters by the Bureau at Albany to send out. The letters were to be sent to localities where there were foreign born people who might need instruction; and schools to be notified by mail. Localities were developing their own local and more complete adult education. Americanization was only one subject in the programs. Organization was not quite as necessary. There had been alien registration notices. Now I had the names and the people involved were to be gotten into classes if interested.

Because of this "office work" for me, I dared to go to Sandy Pond and take Aunt Minnie with me. I did not dare to take her over to the cottage but rented one at Greene Point. I think she appreciated it for she liked the change in scenery and the pain was the same anywhere. Shortly after I knew her problem, I had driven her to Walton and Downsville so that she'd have a chance to see her old home and her friends. Propped up by pillows in the back seat she still had a tough time getting home, but she had grit. We never told her. We never really knew if she guessed. In late

September, near her birthday, Jan was nearly at the point of exhaustion. I told her at 741 Maryland Avenue to go to Westcott Street, take her time and have a good lunch away from things. She had ordered, when I had to call her. She ran all the way back but was in time to be with Aunt Minnie when she passed on. It was less than three months after the two mothers had gone.

After Aunt Min and I had been to the doctor's office, she had said to me to bring a lawyer to the house for she wanted to make a will. Mr. Charles Sheridan had helped me with my mother's estate so I thought of him. He was the father of Frank's friend Charlie, who had spent some time with us at Sandy Pond. I went into the kitchen to lave them alone to talk. Finally they called me in. Mr. Sheridan said, "Miss Holmes wants me to draw up a will leaving all to you and as she decides, she will instruct you what to do with it. She feels there is little estate to think of anyway." He did not like the idea, he said, as the relatives might object. She said, "I haven't the strength to do anything else right now. Grace will carry it out." I did.

On a recent trip to Albany to a staff meeting I had sensed that changes were due. The war was over. I had been borrowed for the duration by Miss Whipple. I wondered about it. Miss Whipple, in the meantime, had resigned and Dr. Ralph Spence was now the head of the Bureau.

Again I was in Syracuse. I had plenty of estate business to take care of and I also needed a hat. I went into the old

Morris Plan Bank in East Fayette Street, of which J. Russell was a Director. As I stepped toward the window I felt as if I were slipping out of consciousness. I had had the same feeling at Maryland Avenue within the month when all went black. I said to the girl, "Can you help me? I feel I'm going to faint." Next thing I knew, I was in a director's chair. My pocketbook was way down on the bank floor and someone was saying, "The color is coming back." When all was O. K., I was still determined to get the hat. There was a hat store next door. I went in. The girl, as she was waiting on me, asked if I was O. K. I told her what had just happened. She said she was a former nurse and asked if she could take my pulse. Then she said, "I will sell you this hat, but then you must go home by taxi and call the doctor." I laughed for I didn't feel it was that serious. However, the medical doctor gave me a hard blow. He told me to resign immediately and take it very easy. My blood pressure was 260 and 120. He seemed concerned. I sent the telegram to the Bureau of Adult Education. But the "floor" had dropped out from under me. I wandered around the house and outside feeling lost. I couldn't sleep. I couldn't relax. I didn't even have the satisfaction of feeling sorry for myself. J. Russell, as always, was very loving and affectionate. I called him my "Rock of Gibralter."

In 1947, we went to California for the first time. The two Russell's and Frank had loved it. I would ask, "What is California like?" But no description was forthcoming which would satisfy me. Somewhere I believe this whole marvelous trip is written up. I must try to find it in the attic.

Well, I did, but found the account was shortened to one state, California, for an Onaway Club paper I was to give. I just took time out to read it. We visited thirty-two states.

Finally, we were home again. J. Russell was back in the store. Frank was still in Japan. We'd had no word to tell us when he could be expected but we were uneasy at times for no mail had come thru for weeks. Then a telegram came from the Pacific Coast asking for a money telegram so he could fly home. Marne Holmes was visiting us. We three were out walking in the evening. As we returned to the house the lights were on upstairs. Strange, I thought, I didn't leave them on. And then hesitantly and then with a shout I yelled, "Frank! It must be!" and started running. "Frank!" I yelled up the stairs and took them with a bound with open arms.

But it was a different Frank. He responded not at all. He was withdrawn and closed in, serious and unsmiling. I fought for composure. What had happened to him? I could not fathom it. Something devastating no doubt of it. There were days and days of silence. No conversation – stolid looks. My heart nearly broke. I didn't know what to do or say to help him. Tears came many a time but I ran down cellar so they wouldn't be seen. I could sense only that those years were too much for him too. A young lad to an adult too fast. What to do? Nothing! Sometimes J. R. and left we were being blamed for something but we couldn't fathom what it was – or perhaps it didn't involve us at all.

There was no ray of light. My love for Frank grew so deeply it hurt. We never did find out just what it all meant but as gradually the situation changed our inner selves sang again. We had Frank, Jan and Howie and two grandchildren, Bobby and Donnie. We were a family again! The world had changed but it wasn't so terribly bad

216

after all. There were all the possibilities ahead for a new start!

And next I come to something I've regretted all my life. We all make those terrible mistakes sometimes and wish our tongue hadn't run away with us. I came home from downtown one day to find Frank moving all his belongings and the furniture he wanted into the N. W. bedroom. Sentimentalist that I was, that had continued to be Russ' room and I had often gone to the doors of his and to Frank's room and imagined the boys to still be there. It seemed to help! Caught off guard, I was furious. Frank unknowingly was upsetting my picture of things. I surprised him by asking what he was doing without asking me. More and more I said, until his expression conveyed to me that I thought he didn't have any part in the house. Flabbergasted I stopped! My mother always said, "Grace doesn't get mad only about once in six years, but once she does, watch out. She says anything that comes into her head and doesn't really mean a word of it." I felt I'd done irreparable damage. In these late years, I've asked Frank if he remembers that instance. He replied that he didn't but I never forgot. I'd always felt home belonged to all of us. I had no intention of dominating but I felt I had.

After the war ended, Frank had played football in Japan to help entertain the troops. We suggested that he go to Paul Smith's for the Syracuse University preseason football practice. He did not seem to have any heart in it but he went. Dad and I drove up to see him once. And then there was an accident. Another player's cleated show hit

Frank in the nose and he hemorrhaged so badly he was brought home. It healed.

Charlie Sheridan and Frank were walking downtown when the blood vessel broke again and Charlie got him into the Good Shepherd Hospital on Marshall Street. Dad and I were sent for. Frank had nose and throat packings with strings attached. He was taken upstairs but again and again the blood vessel broke open. Soon he was told to lay on his back without moving for twenty-four hours. Dad set by his bed in the hospital in order to grab him if he moved in his sleep. Frank was wonderful! This time the healing held. But Frank had a severe disappointment. S. U. did not feel it safe for him to play on the team again. It was a blow for me too as I saw too keenly how unhappy Frank was. Dad and I felt deeply for him. Our two sons had been on the Syracuse University football teams, but now that was over.

I feel it takes real courage to return to college after such a devastating break as a war, but Frank had the courage. I had often wondered what Frank's choice of vocation would be. He came into the kitchen one day. He said he'd made up his mind to graduate and then get his M. A. degree and possibly later to go on to a Ph. D. perhaps at another college. He might like to teach. His field would be Business Management thru the College of Business Administration. I was both amazed at his ambition and delighted. It was entirely his decision. J. Russell and I had had almost too much of parental planning in our lives. We endeavored to let our children find their own direction.

During the summer, Frank and Chick Lewis, traveling by car, went west to California, camping most of the way. At college, Frank had met a lovely young girl whom I had heard about but never had seen. He became deeply enamored. He tried to tell me about her but somehow my response was inadequate. I failed him at this point. Though I did suggest that he follow her to her home. Perhaps then things would change for him. He came back refreshed with the scenery, the adventurous experiences with the whole trip, and released from his heart the absorption in the young lady.

Janet and Howie and family were full of plans to build a home of their own. Land was purchased one and a half miles beyond Fayetteville. Howie had wanted to enlist but was keenly disappointed when told he had not passed the physical. Bobby was in school. I remember Bob taking his first steps when the Wells' lived on Strong Avenue. And here comes their special story. Janet was a Paine. She married a Wells and went to live on Strong Avenue.

The three family house on Maryland Avenue had been sold and the Wells rented until their house was complete enough to move into. A water douser found water for them. That was an interesting experience for all of us. We all tried it out with varied success. Anyway, a spring was located, one still furnishing water with never a sign of going dry. Bob was born on July 21, 1938. Don arrived November 2, 1944, and Ken made a three-some on January 8, 1951. The country life has been excellent for all of them even though as near as ten miles away, it often seemed quite a distance. The house grew as fast as Howard's energies could be used. He had some help but mostly it was due to Howie.

J. Russell was chosen a delegate to the American Legion Convention in Los Angeles, California, in 1950, from the local Post 41. Janet was with her family and getting along in fine shape. J. Russell wavered around about going until I didn't know just what was to happen. Frank was very busy with college. Being so uncertain about going, nothing was said to either Frank or Jan. Frank went off to college one morning. Suddenly, as per usual, J. R. said, "Get your things packed!" When Frank came home, the suitcases were by the door ready to leave the next day. No wonder he looked at them in such consternation and amazement! I had fought an inner battle about leaving Frank to shift for himself so soon after his return home and experienced a sense of nervous trepidation about the whole thing. J. R. said, "Frank will be O. K. He can eat at college or at the Fraternity Phi Kappa Psi." He added, "He has money of his own. It will only be six weeks." This was a trip that I did not start out on happily. I kept thinking of Frank. However, we were off and nothing more could be done about it except write home.

We took a different route than the first time. There were not such marked changes in scenery until we reached Colorado Springs, The Garden of the Gods and climbed Pikes Peak. It is going to be impossible to write of the trips west in all detail in this already lengthy narration. Somewhere in the attic at 935 Comstock, the trip write-ups and the letters are still available if needed. This time I had with me a camera to take colored pictures. They follow us along pretty well. We reached Bryce National Park high in the mountains with its landscape of fantastic pink, white and yellowish rock carvings. The day was very cloudy overhead with moments of brilliant sunshine. I raced around taking pictures when I could. We planned to sleep in the Rambler overnight until we were warned by the park attendant that the blackening clouds meant snow and 25 degree weather; there was no heat available anywhere – we had better drive on. It was nearing dark so we drove rapidly toward Orderville, Utah.

Before long the car started making an unusual racket, not at all normal to our experience. It grew louder as we went along, but the car continued to run which was fortunate as all was dark, lonely and strange. As we went thru the village of Orderville, we sounded like a threshing machine. Pulling up in front of the only garage, we met Mr. William Heaton for the first time. He and his brother, LeGrand Heaton ran the place. Mr. Heaton was busy but made the casual remark that he thought he knew what the trouble was. Later when the car was elevated, he said the trouble was the differential and it was a wonder we had arrived there. He had nothing to fix it but would phone to Salt Lake City, 250 miles away and have one brought down on the truck in the morning. We stayed in a motel run by Orson Young, a grandson of Brigham Young, the pioneer settler (Mormon) in Salt Lake City. Mrs. Young taught school. Each inhabitant seemed to have a particular job to do outside of home. All were of the Mormon faith. That night began six and a half days of now happy memories. The village adopted us. We were met on the streets and asked if we were the people whose car broke down and were stranded in their village. Grace Heaton, William's wife, ran the post office; Burke Sorenson and wife the restaurant; Mr. and Mrs. Hans Chamberlin, the grocery store and LeGrand Heaton's sister made jewelry from the stones and metals in the area and repaired watches. We met the aged mother in her 90's who had her picture taken with us.

Mr. Sorenson invited us to ride with him to a soft coal mine run by a man who was remarkable for his garrulousness, wit and humor. The Young's directed us to

221

Red Canyon where two rock mountains came together in a cleft so close that only with difficulty could we slip thru the towering sides of red and yellow. There was an eerie strangeness about the landscape that isn't easy to forget. The weather was hot. We sat in the front yard on Mr. Young's chairs. The Hans Chamberlin's sent over ice cream to our surprise. Nellie Heaton took us to a villager who was an artist and an art teacher in the Salt Lake City University. Real nice things kept happening every day.

On one occasion I took a stroll over to the post office. A big expensive car came down the street with two nice looking, well-dressed men in it. They stopped next to me and both got out. One started talking to me asking questions about the village, the people. I got the idea immediately and, inwardly amused, let him ramble on and on in an effusive manner. He shook hands with me finally and said he was running for office on the ---- ticket. That I had already guessed. When he asked me if I would vote for him, I couldn't hold back the fun any longer. "I'm glad to meet you," I said, "But I don't live here. I live in New York State." The other man roared with laughter and said, "Wait until I tell that one to the boys." I went on down the street laughing.

Salt Lake City garage sent down a repair kit for the differential but we were told it had been ground to bits by our driving. As the Rambler was fairly ne, the garage felt it must have had a flaw in it. Mr. Heaton phoned to Los Angeles. Nowhere could he locate one so finally he called Kenosha, Wisconsin, to fly one to us and we waited. The stay was delightful and the people so friendly. William Heaton and Grace drove us to the north rim of the Grand Canyon, one hundred miles away on a Sunday. As Mr. Heaton had had no sleep, he had Russell take the wheel coming back. As we slowed in the forest area of the Lodge for dinner, Russell whispered to me, "How do you stop this car?" It was different from ours.

One day Mr. Young was not at the motel. It was nearly noon and no work had been done in any cabins. No beds freshly made. As I was wondering about this, a woman came into the yard and said she knew Mr. Young had gone to the canning. Puzzled, I asked a few questions. In the next town all surplus food was being made ready for the winter, at church direction. All the families raised the food, decided how much they needed; all else was made ready for those who were sick or unable to carry on the crop raising. No one is left in need. All shared. After the canners left, those who were left at home were to help get the normal tasks done. I was intrigued. I had nothing special to do. I offered to help and together we cleaned and made up all the cabins and carried the laundry to the tubs. When Mr. Young returned all was done and the clothes hung up to dry.

A friend asked me on our return home if they hadn't been trying to convert us to Mormonism. I felt inwardly indignant. "No," I said, "No word was ever mentioned. It was I who finally asked Mr. Young about the religion and he gave me some books to read."

On the morning of the last day, there was a knock at the cabin door at 6:30 A. M. and we were told that if we came to the garage our car would be ready. The part had been flown to Salt Lake and brought down by truck during the night. Mr. LeGrand Heaton after working all night, stayed up to get us started on our way. He knew that Russell was anxious to arrive at Los Angeles, as he was a delegate to the American Legion Convention to be held there, and there was little time left to finish the journey.

We started out and were coming down the long, winding road into Zion Canyon when the car stopped and it seemed very heated and refused to go. It was unbearably hot, but we had to wait until an infrequent car came along. It contained a young couple whom Russell hailed but who seemed noticeably afraid of us. Perhaps they had heard tales of hold-ups, but they were persuaded to carry me back to Orderville to the garage, now twenty-five miles away.

As I arrived, LeGrand Heaton was just going home to milk the cows and go to sleep. He said he thought he knew what the trouble was and if I would wait until he milked the cows, he would go back with me. On the way he said, "Keep talking about something or sing to me to keep me awake," and that I did. He fixed the car in no time. He said he had no experience with Ramblers and had tightened something too tight. The car had heated and set. Then he felt that as long as he was there, he'd better stay to show us the Canyon as there were many interesting places and stories about them that the tourists never saw or heard. He stayed with us all day and we made arrangements to sleep in the camping area in our car. We hoped he could return home without my singing to him. A remarkable thing about his episode was the charges with all the phoning, the cost of getting the part, etc. were only $25 and they refused more. Russell said he would not have been surprised if it had been $200.

All these very wonderful friends still correspond with me, especially at Xmas, except Mr. William Heaton who was crushed by a car coming off the overhead lift and killing him. On a subsequent trip, we found LeGrand running the garage alone and Mr. Young had built a large, very modern and attractive motel with a swimming pool. We were greeted royally. Several years later, my daughter, Howie and Kenny stopped over night and met our friends.

We arrived in Los Angeles in time for the Legion affairs. I spent the time that Russell was in the parade with Emma Lou Shaw, a former member of the Theosophical Lodge in Syracuse. She made an appointment for me with Hereward Carrington for one morning. I have a book which he gave me, one of his writing. He was the author of several, among them co-author with Sylvan Muldoon of *The Case for Astral Projection*. I had told him of my, to me, extraordinary happening at the time of my son's death which he did not think too unusual and of my second experience of this kind following the first. He was quite interested. Emma Lou Shaw also took me to a lecture by Manly P. Hall. Over 2,000 people attended. Emma Lou and I sat on the floor near the door. There were no seats left. We visited the Philosophical Research Building in which Manly P. Hall has amassed a tremendous library of books on philosophy, ancient wisdom, religions, and occult phenomena – some so old, rare and scarce as to be locked in special cases under glass.

Russell and I also went to see Helen Stark, a lecturer and former member of Syracuse Lodge. Much more could be told of this trip and of the six we took west by car, getting into 48 of the 50 states and the edges of Canada and Mexico. There are many slides at home, letters and accounts to follow us on these trips. Eventually we went to see Frank and Johanne when they lived in Berkeley, in Albany twice and to Stamford. Our seventh trip was by airplane, an astro-jet – when Frank received his Ph. D. degree.

When we arrived home from the American Legion trip, Frank seemed quite happy and I had a feeling he had managed all right. I was relieved, as I'd thought a great deal about his shifting for himself those six weeks. He had worked at Syracuse University's registrar for the fall term and met a fellow worker Johanne Thompson. Frank brought her to the house to meet us and before long, we were in the excitement of the second wedding – Jan's and now Frank's. It was held in St. Paul's Episcopal Church in Syracuse and a reception was held at her Grandmother's (Mrs. Maude Irvine). It was a very happy day. Only when it was all over, when I returned home and looked into Frank's room, it came to me with tremendous impact that seldom would Frank be back with us again. Russell and I were alone.

Chapter II

Frank and Johanne lived in University housing on East Colvin Street. Later they moved to North Burdick Street in Fayetteville and after Frank received his M. A. degree, moved to Berkeley, California, to get his Ph. D. Young Russ, the IV, and Linda Sue were born while they were in Fayetteville. When Tom was born, they lived in Albany, California, and J. Russell and I raced out to Berkeley to care for Russ and Linda while Johanne was in the hospital, but we did not make it in time. We had arrived in El Paso, Texas, when the word arrived. Mr. Paine had had a fifty day session in the VA hospital and did not feel too well.

Somewhere along this time, I joined the Co-Masonic Order and took the first three Masonic degrees in Buffalo, New York. It is an Order for both men and women essentially the same as male masonry, international but not too well known. Later I took the 18th degree at Cleveland, Ohio. During a visit to Buffalo, Mr. Sri Ram, President of the international Theosophical Society, led the ritual that brought me into the Esoteric Section.

At the time of the finding of the Dead Sea Scrolls, I became deeply interested in the Essences and read everything I could find out about them in books and articles. I was interested in the Qumram Monastery and the thought that Jesus was part of that order. Writing to New York City to get additional material from Samuel Weiser's book concern at 845 Broadway, dealer in rare, out of print books, and new ones, I secured a second-hand pamphlet about the Essenes which I found had the name of Hubert Harisin in it and his address in Redlands, California, Route 2, Box 80. I wrote this gentleman about the pamphlet and he replied, starting an animated correspondence on the Essenes and their teachings. He proved to be a modern-day Essenic Minister of the Essenic Order. I was thrilled. On one of our trips west, we stopped to see Lavinia and Hubert in their modest home which had acres of orange trees nearby. We slept in our Rambler car bed in their yard. On another trip west, we again stopped and I was initiated in the Essenic Order taking the first degree of which there are three. I wished to continue but because of Russell's physical difficulties we never got there again. Correspondence continued however.

May I step backward in time for a few minutes? I have neglected to say that we had five trips in the winters to Florida, similar to the California ones, liking Miami, Homestead and Key West the best, largely due to the swimming opportunities in ocean waters, the sunshine, the warmth. So many special stories could be told of these trips also. On the return from the fifth trip to Florida, a phone call came saying that we had better come right up to Sandy Pond. Our camp could not be seen anywhere. We went and not a thing was left, whatever had been left in the cabin, two boats on the banks and all but one tree, a willow leaning dejectedly into the water of the pond. We were told that a seventy-five mile an hour wind and rainstorm had swept the lake. We hired a boat and went around the shores of Sandy Pond twice but no a piece of wood or anything showed us what had happened to the building. This was in the early 1950's, I think. We found no one who had any idea about it either.

For the next few years in the summers, we stayed home taking picnic trips around the area and often skirting the shores of Lake Ontario half hoping for another place at a small price. Most were packed closely together and that we did not like. Perhaps it was 1959 when we had a phone call from Sarah Marsh who had a cottage at Fair Haven, telling us that there was a place for sale which she thought we might like. It was off North Lake Street and bordered on the State Park. We went up to see it and purchased it that very day. J. Russell has loved it and looks forward to it every summer. We have the big Lake Ontario and Little Sodus Bay, the Park and the seawall to look at out of our windows and all the fun and attractions that go with camping.

Another addition to this I would like to insert here. My being president of the Theosophical Lodge in Syracuse brought a number of guests to my home - those who visited Syracuse to give public lectures. Among them have been Ernest Wood, Alvin Boyd Kuhn, Mr. and Mrs. John Coates of England, Clara Codd, Dora and Fritz Kunz and others. Two stories I want to tell: Clara Codd from South Africa and England, writer of a number of books, asked one day about the American Indians and was surprised that a reservation was nearby. I drove her there and as we went thru the area, she said, "But I don't understand, where are the wigwams?"

Sri Ram from India, a spiritual, gentle being, stayed here for five days while lecturing downtown. I took him for a ride thru our valleys and hills to the south of the city. It was fall and the leaves were at their most gorgeous coloring over which he exclaimed. When I was trying to keep the household work going, he asked, "When you get thru with your duties, may we go to see the leaves again?" I finished the washing and we went down thru Nedrow and to the south. He sat very quietly drinking it all in, and then said, "Do they do this *every* year?" with a note of surprise in his voice. When I said yes, he answered that he had been around the world many times lecturing but had never been in the right place at the right time to see anything so wonderful before.

While I am at it, I wish to speak of seeing Krishnamurti and Anni Besant in Chicago at the Stevens Hotel in 1927. A number of the Lodge members went to this well-publicated event, including my mother and myself. The whole of the Stevens Hotel was taken up by Theosophists. Krishnamurti spoke to an intense crowd. In Ojai, California, when I went to get acquainted with Krotono, the Esoteric Center of the T. S., I had the opportunity of hearing him again while seated on the ground in a natural amphitheater. He was so unassuming and yet so profound. His message is still ahead of our times.

Paul Galloway, our assistant manager at the Syracuse Victory Soap Corp. at 252 West Washington Street, of which J. Russell was president, manager and treasurer, and I was secretary, served a time in the Army in the Second World War during which I was at the store each day and at times helped with the delivering. It was largely wholesale trade with a smaller part retail. Paul returned. He managed things for us when we went on trips. J. Russell was very fond of him and felt he was another son. He eventually willed the store and contents to him which Paul never knew. But one day Russell called me in alarm, "Paul's gone," he said. "Gone where?" I asked. "Left us," he said, "No advance notice. No word. Gone to work elsewhere." Russell seemed quite crushed. I rushed downtown. He was visibly upset but finally said, "Do you know what I'd like to do? Dissolve the corporation and retire." I asked, "Think we can manage?" So off he went to a lawyer and I helped full-time for two months until he had sold all the remaining goods and furnishings.

In my wandering around I'd met Carleise Pike and knew she ran the Pioneer Workshop for Handicapped People on Catawba Street. We took our benches and long desk over to her for use in the workshop. When delivery was made, I saw beautiful oil paintings lining the upper part of the room. I exclaimed, "My! I wish I could paint like that!" Thus I met Ray Bolles, who became my teacher for the next several years. I'd tried two years of correspondence school lessons with Art Instruction of Minneapolis, Minnesota, but working in a group was much more pleasant and more satisfactory. Later, Ray Bolles taught at Mickey Cimbal's on her glassed-in porch. One of the summers, Ray and his wife, Bess, went with three of us for a few days stay in Rockport and Gloucester. We saw a demonstration painting by Harry Ballinger and when going to Emile Gruppe's studio, he remembered me from meeting me at Crandon Beach in Miami when I leaned up against a palm tree for three hours straight and watched him paint a beach scene which shortly sold for $350.00.

This trip is written up in the notebook of "The Left Over Group."

On one of these trips west, we stopped at Seattle, Washington to see Dorma and Gene Coley. While there a telephone call from Jan informed us that Bob and Ann were married in a simple, pretty house wedding at the Wells. Very recently, Robin, their oldest child was ten years old. I could scarcely believe it. How time moves along. Bob and Ann have seven children now, two boys and five girls: Robin, Robert, Richard, Randy, Carol Lee, Susan and Terry Lynn.

After the Ph. D. degree, Frank and family moved to College Park, Hyattsville (7214 Windsor Lane), Maryland, and he is still Professor of Business Management at the University of Maryland. Their beautiful home has recently been enlarged. The three children are now fifteen, thirteen, and eight and a half

My interest in art continued. I was no completely out of Adult Education work. I retired to have time for interests of my own. Besides landscape and seascape in oil, I took up portraiture in pastels with Robert Hofmann at 100 Stafford Avenue, Eastwood, and continued regularly until I had pneumonia in 1966. Since then it has been quite irregular. I became a member of the Onondaga Art Guild, The Associated Artists, and the Oswego Art Guild. There have been exhibits in many places also in prejudged shows. Today there are seven on exhibition at their request at the new Gateway Building. During the years, I have taught painting at the Pioneer Workshop, at the Salvation Army, to grace Egelston's Group in her home, to private pupils at Fair Haven, t the Consolidated Industries of Syracuse and Onondaga County, and am now in the second year at the Mental Health Rehabilitation Center of the Veteran's

Administration in the Gateway Building, which is under the direction of Dr. Black, Dr. Stabile and Mrs. McCormick.

At present, a group of us take more advanced painting under Don Centrone at the Betts Library on South Salina Street. Because of J. Russell's increasing physical problems I'm at home more now than I've ever been.

Don Wells, Jan and Howie's middle boy has just graduated from college on January 27, 1968 and enters Officers Candidate School at Newport, Rhode Island, on March 16th. Ken is getting near to the end of high school. Howie was Scout Master of Troop 41 until recently. Don and Ken are both Eagle Scouts plus. Howie, Jan, Don, Ken, and Grace Wells, Howard's Mother, still live at 8064 East Genesee Street, Fayetteville, New York.

Before I end this, having brought myself pretty much up to date, I return to Ephraim Paul Holmes whom once we wheeled around in a doll carriage. He is now a 4 Star Admiral in Command of the Atlantic Fleet and the NATO Atlantic Fleet. How proud we are of you and your career, Paul.

How many things I might have added to this, I really don't know. Perhaps some day there will have to be an addenda.

As one gets a bit older one can look back at a busy life and inwardly say, "What are the problems and lessons of a life 'in pursuit of Leo?'" In a measure, I've faced them all, being uplifted by some and chastened by others. A too sensitive nature, suffering from self-consciousness from the beginning, had to learn to face life unafraid and with courage; had to learn that all that comes is beneficent, even when it seems most difficult; that if we look with an infinite viewpoint instead of a narrow one, that all is a tremendous unity and each is in his proper place to work toward greater Divine understanding.

February 14, 1968

Grace Holmes Tobey Lockwood Paine
1896 - 1989

Frank W. Tobey

James Russell Paine, II

Frank, Russ, and Janet at Sandy Pond

Janet and Howard on their wedding day

Janet and her oldest son Bob at Sandy Pond, 1939

Grace's children Russ, Janet, Frank, and grandson Bob

Janet, Grace, J. Russell, Russ, and Frank Paine, 1944

Janet and Howard with their sons Bob, Don, and Ken

*Grace with her son Frank and
grandchildren Russ, IV and Linda Sue*